Anabaptism

From its Rise at Zwickau to its Fall at Münster 1521–1536

Richard Heath

SOJOURNER
PRESS

Editing by Hunter Hays

Cover design by Sojourner Press
Foreground picture: engraved portrait of Balthasar Hubmaier by Christoffel van Sichem 1581–1658. Public Domain.
Background picture: "Vier putti met druiven" by Anonymous (between 1725 and 1774). Public Domain.

ISBN 978-1-960255-08-2 (Paperback)

ISBN 978-1-960255-09-9 (Epub)

Printed in the United States of America
Sojourner Press
Raleigh, NC
sojournerpress.org

For bulk, special sales, or ministry purchases, please contact us at sales@sojournerpress.org.

Contents

Introduction to the Revised Edition

Richard Heath (1831–1912) was an English author and journalist known for several historical and biographical accounts he wrote, including *Historic Landmarks in the Christian Centuries* (1882) and *The English Via Dolorosa* (1893). He also contributed articles and reviews for various journals, and the focus of his work may be described as centering on Christian social activism in the late 19th century.

Anabaptism: From its Rise at Zickau to its Fall at Münster 1521–1536 was published as part of a collection of Baptist manuals designed to provide historical and biographical background to the development of European Baptists. It is a highly valuable resource thanks to Heath's painstaking attention to detail and ability to make much of the historical resources that were available to him. His work shows a determined pursuit of the causes and instigators of the Anabaptism movement, and a sincere interest in a fair exposé of what he terms, the "Poor Man's Faith."

In this revised edition, I have updated the formatting to help readers follow along more easily. Antiquated terminology is smoothed over while retaining the sense of the original author's work. I have also updated minor spelling issues where appropriate, and updated the format of some Scripture references. This revised edition offers a highly valuable resource for tracing the roots of Anabaptism as well as a riveting description of notable events in the formation of the movement.

Hunter Hays, 2023
Raleigh, NC

Preface

Injustice—religious, social, political—having made Anabaptism, strove to destroy not only its confessors, but all Anabaptist writings, thus rendering well-nigh impossible any full and true account of the rise, course, and ruin of the movement. The modern historical spirit has, however, resulted in the collection of a number of documents which throw increased light on early Anabaptism. Unfortunately these documents are mostly from hostile sources, consisting to a great extent of the judicial examinations of the Anabaptist prisoners, whose answers were forced out often by, or in terror of, the rack, and always under mental torture. Of the writings of the early Anabaptists during the period here treated there are very few now extant.

Although the size of this book enforces the utmost brevity, care has been taken to make the best use possible of the results of the industry of the German collectors and historians. In acknowledging my obligations, I would mention first of all the works of C. W. Cornelius. The second volume of his *Geschichte des Münsterischen Aufruhrs* throws much light on the early movements of Anabaptism, and the subject is treated in a remarkably sympathetic manner. His *Berichte der Augenzeugen über das Münsterische Wiedertäuferreich* gives a number of documents relating to the Anabaptist Kingdom at Münster, and a critical account of the sources of its history. Beck's collection of documents entitled *Die Geschichtsbücher der Wiedertäufer* is a truly monumental work; the results so far as they relate to the Tyrol and Moravia have been worked out by J. Loserth in two studies: *Der Anabaptismus in Tirol* and *Der Communismus der Mährischen Wiedertäufer*. These works have been the chief sources of the chapter on the Anabaptists of the Tyrol and

Moravia. Dr. Keller's book, *Ein Apostel der Wiedertäufer*—the biography of Hans Denck—contains summaries of the writings of the most original thinker among the early Anabaptists. This book and Dr. Keller's *Geschichte der Wiedertäufer* have been much consulted. The difference in the tone of these two works with regard to Anabaptism is a striking testimony to its intrinsic worth, and encourages the belief that the more its history is carefully and critically studied, the more it will emerge from the dark fog of prejudice in which it has been enveloped. Another work from which I have gleaned valuable matter with reference to the literature of the Münster movement is Bouterwek's *Literatur und Geschichte der Wiedertäufer*. Egli's works, *Die Züricher Wiedertäufer* and *Die St. Gallen Täufer*, have been the main source of the facts about Swiss Anabaptism. Röhrich's *Geschichte der Strassburgischen Wiedertäufer*, Hoekstra's *Beginselen en leer der oude Doopsgezinden*, Ten Cate's works on the Dutch Mennonites, Dr. J. P. Muller's *Mennoniten in Ostfriesland*, and Frau A. Brons' *Ursprung und Schicksale der Taufgesinnten oder Mennoniten*, have all been drawn upon, besides other sources given at the end of each chapter. Janssen's great work on the *History of the German People since the Middle Ages* has afforded both light and many valuable facts. That a great dignitary of the Roman Catholic Church should take any but the ordinary view of the Münster Kingdom was not to be expected, seeing that even advanced and sympathetic writers do not challenge the dubious character of the history. But that this Münster story, which so terribly befouls the Poor Man's Faith, and pillories him as a fool and a fanatic, should so readily be accepted by the learned of all sects and parties, and that even in an age which has done its best by remorseless criticism to destroy the bases of the Poor Man's Faith, is for me a most portentous fact.

The term "Anabaptism" cannot be limited to its strict meaning of second or adult baptism, for it represents historically a movement having for its aim social and political as well as religious reform. This use of the word in a wider and in a more limited sense, undoubtedly perplexes the subject; but it is impossible entirely to get rid of the difficulty, for the religious movement to which the term strictly belongs is, all through the period here treated, more or less blended with the wider social and political movement.

For any freedom from verbal error attained in the text, as well as for the clearing up of doubtful points, I am greatly indebted to the suggestions of the Editor of this series, and to Dr. J. P. Muller, pastor of the Mennonite community at Emden. I also heartily thank my friends Constance Garnett, Maurice Adams, and Henry Deacon for similar helpful criticism. The Baptist Union, in accordance with its principles, leaving me in full possession of freedom of conscience and freedom of thought, I remain alone responsible for what is said throughout this book.

1

Preludes to Anabaptism

1

In the year in which Luther appeared before the Diet of Worms (1521), certain reformers arose in Zwickau, a town in Saxony, on the high road between Bavaria and Silesia, teaching a different doctrine from that of Luther. They spoke of an inner life, of a knowledge of and friendship with God, possible to all who would give themselves to Christ and do His will. Merely believing the Gospel was true could, they said, save no one; faith must be preceded by repentance and followed by good works. Nicolaus Storch, a clothmaker, Marx Stübner, a student, and Thomas Münzer, a priest who had followed Luther and had been a preacher of his doctrine, were the leaders. Harbingers of the great Anabaptist movement, two of these men had ties with the lands in which the Hussite doctrine had been powerful. Storch finally vanishes in Silesia, whence he apparently came. Münzer, at Prague, claimed to be the successor of Ziska.[1] There is probably truth in the statement that the Anabaptists obtained part of their doctrine from the Bohemian Brethren. They felt and thought as the sects that sprang from Huss, and were divided, as they were, on the right of Christians to use the sword.

Luther gives the idea that these three Zwickau reformers were not of one mind. With reference to their visits to him, he said, "Klaus Storch in a general way contradicted Marco and Thomas, and talked about nothing

---

1. Leader of the militant Hussites.

but infant baptism." However, these three men would not have been drawn together and have worked together had they not been essentially one. All Europe was talking of the Reform of Religion; to these men it appeared that Truth ought to be the criterion of that reform, and in seeking Truth and proclaiming it there ought to be sincerity. They agreed with the rest of the Reformers that the standard of Truth was the Bible, and that things must be reformed by the Word of God which it contained; but no one, they contended, could rightly understand the Scriptures unless he was taught by the Holy Spirit. To everyone a measure of that Spirit was given, but only to those who faithfully listened to its voice in their hearts would light arise as to the true meaning of the Scriptures. And only those would affect a true Reformation who were obedient to the commands of Christ. Now one of these commands was Baptism, but baptism according to the New Testament must be preceded by repentance, conversion, and faith. Therefore, infant baptism was worse than useless, and in the reformation of religion it was one of the main corruptions to be removed.

To witness against justification by faith as then too commonly understood, that is, by a faith in which the devils share; to affirm the necessity of the help of the Holy Spirit in seeking God's Word in Holy Scripture; to protest against the practice of infant baptism, these were the main points of the testimony of the prophets of Zwickau. For such they were called from their reliance upon an inner illumination given by God, through the Holy Spirit, to those who lived in obedience to the commands of Christ. Opposition arose and there were tumults in Zwickau, and the authorities seem as usual to have imprisoned the persecuted rather than the persecutors. The new teachers accordingly went on to Wittenberg, where they arrived two days after Christmas, 1521, and found a favorable reception. Luther was in the Wartburg; Carlstadt was prepared for a further advance in the Reformation at Wittenberg; Melancthon was in so open a state of mind that he had Stübner in his house for the next six months; while Cellarius, coming forward to defend Lutheran views, avowed himself conquered and joined the prophets. Under such circumstances Wittenberg came rapidly under the influence of the latter. The trend of thought in Germany was with them. The most cultured minds of the age had attained, as they supposed, to the limits of ordinary knowledge, and wished to master the secrets of the invisible world.[2]

A mystical spirit was abroad, making men unusually interested in the idea of immediate revelation. The Wittenberg people streamed to the meetings held by the prophets, where in simple language they were urged to think of the salvation of their souls and to turn away from all human wisdom, the only true knowledge being the gift of God. This depreciation of human learning was all the more striking as there hardly ever was a time in which learning was more prized. Under the new teaching the reaction at Wittenberg was such that George More, the rector of the City school, advised all his pupils to learn a handicraft, and Carlstadt betook himself to the workshops to gather true knowledge from men who understood life and were unperverted by sophistical learning. Perhaps in these conversations he was asked why he did not follow the example of the biblical reformers—Hezekiah and Josiah. At any rate, Carlstadt was soon leading the people in clearing the Wittenberg churches of all objects of superstition or idolatry.

The Elector of Saxony, Frederick the Wise, let the iconoclasts have their way; his simple, straightforward nature evidently saw truth in the new teaching. Melancthon alarmed, wrote anxiously both to Luther and to Frederick: Luther, he said, must come back.

The Elector doubted it, thought no good would come of discussions. "If these men from Zwickau are right," he declared, "I will not consider brother or mother, but suffer what has to be suffered. The wisest thing

---

2. Nine of the German Universities were founded between 1450–1506. Boys of twelve matriculated, and at fifteen were Masters of Arts; at seventeen youths were lecturers; at twenty-one young men were professors; at twenty-seven one became Rector of the University of Vienna. Old men, even men of high position, as abbots, provosts, canons, and princes, came to the classes, all eager to learn. Women also were smitten with the same desire, and several were even distinguished for great learning.

is to let the people alone." Referring to the prophets he said earnestly to his council, "If my dear God has given poverty to me and my brother, as soon as I understand this is so, rather than knowingly act against my God, I will take a staff in my hand and go away."

Luther quitted the Wartburg and returned to Wittenberg, March 8, 1522. What line he meant to take with the men from Zwickau was evident from a letter written to Melancthon, and dated January 17th. "So far," he wrote, "he had heard nothing of these preachers but what Satan might say and do. Let, them prove their mission either by authority from the Church, or by miracles. How do they know children do not believe? Faith is not always active, as, for example, when we are asleep. Faith may exist in a child, and yet be dormant. Besides, may not the faith of others be efficacious on their behalf? This universal agreement of the whole Church about infant baptism is a special miracle; even the heretics acknowledge it. To deny it is to deny the Church itself. Do we bring to Christ more than He has already said that He is willing to receive? Moreover, what is not against Scripture is in harmony with Scripture, and the Scripture with it."

When Luther reached Wittenberg, neither Storch, Stübner, nor Münzer was in the city. Stübner hastened back to encourage his friends and defend the cause. A meeting was arranged; Cellarius came with Stübner, and Melancthon with Luther. The latter heard Stübner out, and then, without giving any proofs, told him that what he had put forward had no support in Scripture, that it was either a fiction of his own imagination or the false delusive promise of the Evil Spirit. Cellarius was indignant at Luther's arrogance, but Stübner quietly said, "Hear, Luther, this will prove to you that I am led by the Spirit of God. You are now inclining to think my doctrine is true." "God punish thee, Satan," cried Luther, and, without further parley, he sent them away. They left in anger, went to Ehrenberg, and wrote an indignant letter. Storch now arrived in Wittenberg, accompanied by Münzer. They went to see Luther, but he regarded them in the same arrogant manner. He finishes a letter to Spalatin with the remark, "So Satan drives men to play his game."

Whether or not an emissary from Storch preached at Cologne, as early as 1521 the Zwickau teaching had a friend there in Gerhard Westerburg. He circulated Storch's writings over the Lower Rhine district. It seems also probable that the Zwickau teaching soon reached Münster, for a Münster prophet in 1534, appealing to a congregation, spoke of some present who had heard "God's Word there as far back as 1524." In the same year Bernard Knipperdolling, a furrier in Münster, went in a Dutch ship with Melchior Hoffmann to Stockholm, and under their influence the people began to break the images.[3] Two years later traces of second or adult baptism appear in the Netherlands, and in East Friesland Anabaptist tendencies are soon seen. Analogous movements appear about the same time in other parts of Germany.

2

The tolerance of the government of Cleve led many refugees for conscience sake to seek an asylum in its territories. Werner von Palent, high bailiff of Wassenberg, sympathized with and protected these exiles. He opened his house for a reformed worship, Kloprys, who had been in prison at Cologne, being chaplain. Vinnen of Diest, Slachtscaep of Tongres, Staprade of Mörs, Roll of Grave, were all fugitives, who, having come into the Wassenberg district, went about preaching and administering the sacraments, forming centers, whence their disciples issued in companies seeking the conversion of the peasants. In the course of three or four years the northern part of the Jülich lands became full of evangelical communities, synods even being held. These preachers were not at that time consciously one with the Zwickau prophets or the Anabaptists; but since they subsequently, as a teaching body, became leaders in the Anabaptist movement, their association and work in Wassenberg is an important point in this history. Kloprys was a Lutheran, Slachtscaep

---

3. Melchior Rinck is included in this tradition, but there is some reason to believe that the names Rinck and Hoffmann refer to one and the same person.

under Zwinglian influence, Vinnen perhaps inclined to anti-Trinitarian views. Roll was the means of uniting all together, so that for the rest of their lives they worked and finally died for the same principles. He spoke, as the prophets of Zwickau, of the union of the soul directly with God through the Holy Spirit. Outward ceremonies he regarded as only aids to memory and testimonies to the great facts of the Gospel. The Apostles heard the words of Christ, but were powerless until they received the Holy Ghost. To seek invisible things by any other means was to pervert the soul. While rejecting infant baptism, he was distinguished by an extraordinary toleration with regard to those who did not see as he did. He would not despise or scorn any of the Reformers, for all have worked with a good intent, each after his own way of thinking, as he after his, that the House of the Lord may at last be perfectly completed. He urged his friends not to give way to hatred or bitterness. If the persecutors knew the true flesh and blood of Christ, they would rather die themselves than blaspheme that which they now in ignorance blaspheme.

The ducal ordinance of 1532, setting up a State Church in Cleve and Jülich, remaining a dead letter, an inquiry was held in all parts of the duchies as to the reasons. This led to the persecution of the Wassenberg preachers and the destruction of their work. Roll, Vinnen, Kloprys, Staprade, Slachtscaep, took refuge in Münster.

This change in the duke of Cleve's policy with reference to religious matters was no doubt one of the results of the great defeat suffered by the People in 1525. The title "Peasant War" is somewhat misleading, for it included many cities and towns. The struggle in 1524–25 was in fact an effort of the People to make the Reformation thorough. The reformation of religion was vitally connected with this great social struggle, and to treat them as wholly distinct movements is to understand neither.

Old things were passing away, some things very bad, some very good; and other things were taking their place, some very good, some very bad. Unhappily the good things that were passing away were the very things that helped the many, while the bad things that took their place worked them harm. Germany had become a center for the trade of the world; its merchants were formed into great commercial companies, whose aim was to monopolize that trade to their own advantage. The silver mines in the Tyrol were so worked as to depreciate the currency. Prices rose, and wages being fixed the poor man grew poorer. On the other hand, the vast development of commerce in certain directions rendered a number of persons much more wealthy. Large fortunes became common, and a magnificent and luxurious style of living set in. This rapidly ruined those who wished to be distinguished, but had not the means. The nobles, to save themselves as long as they could from bankruptcy, became more and more exacting to the peasants. And in this they were assisted by the gradual substitution of the Roman law for the old Teutonic laws and customs.

Moral corruption accelerated the general breakup. The rapid success of a few individuals in a class ruined the morality of the whole class. Men fell into illegitimate ways of making money, especially gambling. Brigandage open and veiled was practiced. The youth of the wealthy classes fell into sybaritic courses; the licentiousness of the middle and upper classes was almost unparalleled.

The immorality of the clergy was notorious; the monasteries and nunneries in deep discredit; bishops led the way in scandalous scenes. Dress was extravagant, drinking outrageous. Speculation, competition, gambling, extravagance, licentiousness, drinking, offered a fine field for the usurer, and people of all classes fell into the bands of the Jews, who extracted exorbitant interest. The cry against them was universal, but it did no good, for the Christian usurers who came in their place were worse. How could the people, with whom alone some virtue remained, respect such a society, and the rulers who fashioned it? The Common Man wished for a clean sweep of the whole of the rulers of Germany, always excepting the Emperor. Their name was legion; not only were there endless numbers of princes, bishops, electors, dukes, landgraves, margraves, counts, lords, abbots, who exercised sovereignty of one sort or another, but the imperial cities were ruled by little oligarchies of old families who, by close combination, possessed as much real sovereignty as any prince. The land was thus broken up into numerous states, great and small, each entrenched against the other; and customhouses, different coinages, bad roads, brigand knights, and bands of robbers divided them still more. The imperial power was weak, and its government did little.

Thus it was that the very idea of Reformation filled Germany with new faith and courage, and thousands of living souls at once rallied to every appeal that came from Wittenberg. But Luther's own sympathies were not democratic. Nevertheless, the movement he began added the last and most active element to the storm that was brewing, and from his disciples came many of its most ardent fomenters and leaders. The people in the towns were discontented enough at their exclusion from their government, but they had such influence through their organization into trade guilds that it was difficult for the authorities to do anything against a determined expression of popular opinion. But in the country the peasants were more at the mercy of the ruling powers, and had no effective means of resisting the efforts that were being made to destroy their position and gradually to establish a new serfdom. At this game many petty sovereigns and powerful landlords had been playing before the introduction of the Roman law in Germany, seeking ceaselessly by pretexts to increase the tithes and compulsory services. But it was difficult under the old German law, which gave the peasants power to protect themselves from encroachments; the new law, however, furnished the lords with just what they needed a legal means which the peasants did not understand, and which, being interpreted by lawyers in the pay of the lords, enabled them to confiscate common-lands, raise new taxes, exact new rents and compulsory services. The forestal rights of the peasants were taken away by new game laws, the chase was entirely forbidden to them, they might not even destroy the game that devastated their fields. And the *landsknechte*, who were employed to maintain this new order of things, and who were among the worst kind of military that ever cursed an unfortunate land, were paid for out of the peasants' labors. Even the Electors themselves in 1502 declared that the poor man was loaded with services, and that he was oppressed by the ecclesiastical and lay tribunals in an exorbitant and absolutely iniquitous manner. When Butzer, more accustomed to self-control than Luther, could, speaking of the way the princes and prelates had oppressed the peasants, use language of such terrific force as the following, we may conceive it was no light evil under which the German peasant groaned, "Up to this" (1526), he said, "they have torn the flesh off his bones, now they would suck the marrow out of his bones. Mark my comparison: if you set a wolf to look after the sheep, or a cat to watch the roast meat, you can easily imagine the result. It is thus the poor man has been taken care of by his masters."

"And there was no helper." The Diet of Worms in 1521 had the best opportunity to effect a reformation in Germany, both in Church and State. Nearly everyone present wished it, even the Emperor himself, and it so happened that at that moment the Pope was a man who truly desired reform—Adrian VI. But the question had been left too long, parties had become too widely separated, too little understood each other; and so in stead of closing the breach, it was left to grow wider every day.

Long before Luther fixed his theses on the church door at Wittenberg, or made his celebrated declaration at the Diet of Worms, the German peasant had been struggling for what was fundamentally the same cause: the setting up of truth and justice as the standard, in place of untruth and injustice sanctioned by law and enforced by power. This popular movement had by the translation of the Bible received a very decisive impetus.[4] For more than a generation the German peoples had had an "open Bible," many translations having preceded that of Luther, and by the invention of printing the Scriptures had been widely disseminated.

It is difficult today to realize the effect this translation of the Bible into German must have had on the disinherited classes throughout the Empire. Here was a book which all the authorities admitted to be the Oracle of God; the most precious treasure the world possessed, and it proved wholly and entirely on the People's side. As they listened to the story of the Exodus, they were encouraged to believe that the time was at hand when those who strove to keep them in bondage would be overwhelmed, as was Pharoah. When in the scathing words of Isaiah and Ezekiel, of Amos and all the prophets, they heard described their own lords, usurers, and monopolist-traders, their luxurious prelates and voluptuous *jeunesse*

---

4. In 1518 it was already reckoned that there were fourteen complete translations of the Bible in High German and five in Low German—Janssen, Vol I, p. 603.

dorée, their hearts must have glowed with the thought that the reappearance of this longhidden volume was a sign that the day of their redemption drew nigh. Here, in what the reformers called "God's Word," they found the bearers of it at all times animating the courage of the down-trodden and the oppressed, and even God Himself was there revealed as suffering with man and bent on his deliverance, "I have seen, I have surely e'en the affliction of My people, and have heard their cry by reason of their taskmasters, for *I know their sorrows*." And in that mysterious way in which the heart of the People is moved at words like these, throb after throb was felt throughout Europe. Thoughts flew and desires were awakened such as no press-laws or customhouses could arrest. The New Testament might be burnt, but the poor in Christendom exclaimed, "He that is mighty hath done unto me great things, and holy is His name." Neither mountains, nor rivers, nor even the North Sea itself could arrest the movement. Special indignation set in against those whose office bound them to be the guardians of the Divine Society; for the people saw that just in proportion to the loftiness of the position of the clergy, they had sold the City of God to "the prince of this world."

In 1476 appeared in Niklashausen "the holy youth" Hans Böhm, a farm servant and herdsman, who was believed to have received a commission from the Holy Virgin. The wrath of God, he said, threatened men especially the priesthood. He called them to repentance, denounced Rome and the clergy. The lords oppressed the people, Emperor and Pope allowed it; but there would soon be neither Pope nor Emperor, neither Prince nor Bishop, nor any rulers temporal or spiritual, for each would be his neighbor's brother. Tolls, services, rents, tithes, taxes—all would be done away with. The fish and the game would be common to all. No clergyman ought to have more than one benefice; and if the clergy did not forthwith amend their lives, the whole world would be made to suffer for their sins. It is needless to add that Hans Böhm's inconvenient prophesying was soon quenched in the flames.

In 1486 an insurrection broke out in Bavaria. In 1491 and 1492 insurrections occurred in the domains of the Prince-Abbot of Kempten.

In 1493 the "Bundschuh"[5] was raised in the diocese of Strassburg. The People demanded the right to tax themselves, each commune to have its own law court, expulsion of the Jews, no priest to have more than one benefice, the year of jubilee to be proclaimed when all debts will be annulled, customhouses and duties to be abolished.

In 1502 the Bundschuh appeared in the diocese of Speyer. The insurgents declared that they had united to abolish the authorities; that they would have no master except the Emperor; that the property of the nobility and clergy would be confiscated; tithes, customhouses, duties, would be done away with; and the waters, forests, fields, pasturage, commons, game, birds, fish would be common to all. As usual, the promoters of the rising found themselves at last in the bands of the executioner.

Still the movement grew both in the width of its aims and in the intensity of the faith that it had a divine source. Failure after failure did not discourage. In 1513 there was another attempt in Baden, but it was nipped in the bud. In 1514 it broke out in Wurtemberg, and was there known as "the Revolt of Poor Conrad," Its aims were the same, but it was not confined to the peasants. The duke put it down in a most sanguinary manner.

In 1517 the "Bundschuh" was again raised in Baden, the whole country from the Black Forest to the Vosges being enveloped in a network of insurrections. Every power, except that of the Emperor, was to be abolished, and no taxes paid except to him and to the Church. As yet, no heretical voice had prompted these insurrections. Their leaders and supporters were all members of the Roman Catholic church.

But after 1521 Hans Böhm's prophecies began to be fulfilled, and the wrath of the People turned especially against the upper clergy, so that the

---

5. The peasants adopted the great laced-up shoe ordinarily worn by the German peasantry as the standard around which they rallied. They called it the Bundschuh (the tied, or laced-up shoe), and carried it at the end of their pikes or painted it on their standards.

things they loved and cherished were torn from them, and what could not be taken was desecrated and ruined.

In May 1524 the first drops of the coming storm fell in Franconia. At the same time there were similar movements in the Black Forest and on the borders of Switzerland, and also in the environs of Nürnberg. Ere long they had run along the Swiss frontier and the Lake of Constance, and were spreading in Elsass, the Palatinate, the Rheingau, Franconia, Hesse, Saxony, and the duchy of Brunswick. In the south they spread to the Tyrol, to the archbishopric of Salzburg, to Carinthia and Carniola. The whole of Upper Germany, except Bavaria, was affected.

The object was a complete social reform: the land to become a communal possession, and means to be taken to render the pecuniary position of all more equal. The insurgents fought, so they said, for the "Holy Gospel." And this is what that expression practically meant:

1. Every commune has the right to choose its own pastor, who ought to teach the true faith without human additions.

2. For his maintenance let there be a tithe on corn, but none on cattle.

3. Every man being redeemed by Christ's blood is a Freeman. We are therefore free and will be free. But this is no reason we should refuse to obey magistrates.

4. The game laws must cease, those only who have bought certain rights being indemnified.

5. Woods and forests taken possession of by any means except fair purchase must be returned to their original owner—the Commune.

6. Compulsory services must not be beyond those borne by our fathers.

7. No services must be demanded beyond those agreed upon.

8. Lands rented too highly must be submitted to the arbitration of irreproachable persons.

9. Justice must be impartially administered.

10. Fields and meadows diverted from the common lands, except by fair sale, must be returned.

11. All confiscation of property on death of owner must be forever abolished.

12. If any of the above articles are contrary to Scripture we will renounce them, or if any according to Scripture have been omitted, we hold ourselves bound to accept and maintain them. The peace of Jesus Christ be with everyone, Amen.

The twelve articles appear in different versions in different places, but are intrinsically the same. They were felt to be just, and many of the richer citizens in the various cities and towns were entirely on the side of the insurgents, and considered the movement the work of God.

Its most ardent apostles were among the poorer parish priests, some of whom openly preached the insurrection in their villages. From them and from monks who had fled their monasteries, the insurgent bands obtained their chaplains, counsellors, chancellors, and captains. Among the more distinguished sympathizers were these reformers: Dr. Balthasar Hubmaier, of Waldshut; Thomas Münzer, one of the prophets of Zwickau; Carlstadt, Luther's old colleague; and Carlstadt's brother-in-law, Dr. Gerhard Westerburg. Hubmaier is said to have written the original twelve articles, and Westerburg wrote those for his district. None of them, however, threw themselves into the movement as Münzer did. He was emphatically the prophet of the insurrection; its spirit of intense animosity against the ruling classes seemed concentrated in him. "Nature," he said, "is dead in me; I am nothing but a principle."

At first the movement carried all before it. The towns became centers of the general insurrection. Nearly all the citizens sided with the peasants, opening their gates at their approach, driving out the old Councils for those of a more democratic character. In March and April, 1525, a wave of destruction swept through the country; churches and abbeys, castles and convents, were wrecked. And so the insurrection grew more and more violent, until at Weinsberg the vengeance treasured up for ages in the heart of the People burst out in fury. Everyone "booted and spurred" was condemned to perish. The cause had to expiate this wild revenge, for almost immediately after the events at Weinsberg the peasants foolishly made a bandit-noble, Gotz of Berlichingen, their commander-in-chief. This man and the bankrupt duke Ulrich of Würtenberg in control of the movement, its ruin was inevitable. It seemed spreading, but there was no longer any unity in it, and it was beaten down in detail. Münzer did all that one man could do, but for his final struggle he could only collect 8,000 men. Against them came the united forces of the rulers of Hesse, Saxony, and Brunswick. The peasants were completely defeated in the battle of Frankenhausen, and a general massacre ensued, 6,000 men being slain (May 15, 1525). Mühlhausen was put to the sack, and 300 persons beheaded. The executioner went about everywhere.

On the 22nd and 30th, Luther wrote to Dr. Johann Rühel on this method of treating the peasants. These two letters throw intense light on the history with which this book deals. In the first, Luther says, "That they proceed with the poor people in so horrifying a manner is truly pitiable. But what can one do? It is necessary, and God also wills to have the people brought into fear and awe." In the second, he says, "They (the peasants) won't listen to what they are told, and are mad, so they must listen to the whip and the whiz of the arquebuse, and serve them right. Let us pray for them that they may obey; if not, there will be little reason to pity them; let the arquebuses whiz among them, otherwise it will be a thousand times worse."[6] Later on, Luther wrote a little book against the

---

6. Luther. Briefe, Sendschreiben und Bedenken gesammeit von W, L. M. de Wette. Vol. II., pp. 666, 669-670. Letters. DCCV. and DCCVII.

Peasants.[7] Having treated of the duty of the authorities, he said, "In the case of an insurgent every man is both judge and executioner. Therefore, whoever can should knock down, strangle, and stab such, privately or publicly, and think nothing so venomous, pernicious, and devilish as an insurgent. It may happen that he who is on the side of the authorities may be killed, but if he fought with the conscientiousness spoken of, he is a true martyr before God. On the other hand, that which perishes on the peasant side is an everlasting hell-brand. Such wonderful times are these, that a prince can merit heaven better with bloodshed than another with prayer."

After this, what could be expected of the princes? Catholic, Zwinglian, or Lutheran, they were one in slaughtering the German people. Philip of Hesse, the Zwinglian, united his army with those of the Archbishop of Treves and of the Bishops of Würzburg and Speyer to stamp out the revolt. Casimir of Brandenburg, the Lutheran, put out in one day the eyes of fifty-seven citizens at Kitzingen, besides causing the fingers of numbers of people to be chopped off. At Rothenburg, where he had given the general in command authority to behead, confiscate, burn or pillage at discretion, a young noble, being led to prison, turned to the crowd, crying, "Help me, brave citizens; help me, Christian brothers." But a voice from the crowd exclaimed, "Friend, the time of brotherhood is passed." Casimir prudently stopped after executing about five hundred persons and taking about 400,000 florins in fines—warned, no doubt, by his brother's pithy remark, "If we exterminate all our people, where shall we get other peasants to live upon?" But Antoine of Lorraine, the Catholic, took little account of such practical considerations. In connection with his campaign against the peasants 20,000 were slaughtered. It is computed by the chronicler Anshelm that 100,000 peasants fell on the field of battle or elsewhere. A circular of Bishop Georg of Speyer computes the number at 150,000.

---

7. Wider die Mordischen und Reubischen Rotten der Bauern. Martinus Luther, Wittenberg, 1525. Sammtlichti Werke, Erlangen, 1826-1828, Vol. XXIV. pp. 228-294.

But, what was worse, the whole German peasantry were permanently degraded. Albert of Prussia (October 30) compelled those of his peasants who had taken part in the revolt to kneel before him in the most humble posture, and, after this was done, caused his artillery to play upon them.

Apparently contradictory words are attributed to Münzer in the agonies through which he had to close his career; but the true spirit of his life comes out in these words, "Our cause is like a grain of wheat, which, when it is cast into the earth, men turn away from as if it would never rise again." Then, identifying himself with the cause, he continued, "I am as yet but in the bud, but have patience—I shall ripen, and the ear will bear both grains and spikelets. The just will gather the fruit, but the spikelets will prick the impious and the tyrants to remote ages."

In this fatal year, and in the midst of these terrible circumstances, Anabaptism first comes into prominence. And the facts rapidly sketched here are a necessary preliminary to the following brief account.

Titles of Works Consulted

- Hast, J.: *Geschichte der Wiedertäufer.*

- Keller, L.: *Geschichte der Wiedertäufer.*

- Cornelius, C. A.: *Geschichte des Lübischen Aufruhrs, Bd. 2.*

- Janssen, J.: *Geschichte des Deutschen Volkes seit dem Ausgang des Mittelalters.*

- Zimmermann, W.: *Allgemeine Geschichte des Grossen Bauernkrieges.*

2

Anabaptism in Switzerland

1

As the great German democratic movement of 1524–25 was dying in agony, its spirit appeared elsewhere. Anabaptism rose out of the ashes of the Peasant War, and recommenced the struggle in a deeper, wider, and more enduring manner. Its first corporate expression was in Switzerland, where, surrounded on three sides by the insurrection, it was safe from destruction when the final blows came. Zürich and St. Gall became the first centers of the Baptist faith.

In the former city, Zwingli, by his talents, gift of oratory, and position as preacher at the cathedral, had so affected the public mind as to induce the civic authorities to accept his theological and ecclesiastical views. He went far beyond Luther in making the Bible the one universal standard of truth on all points. With Luther all must be given up that the Bible condemned; with Zwingli all that it did not expressly command. Luther's sacramental views he repudiated, regarding Baptism and the Lord's Supper simply as signs and not necessary to salvation. The apparent thoroughness of Zwingli's reforming zeal had attracted a number of active minds to Zürich, and the city had become a focus of reform—religious, social, and political. Before 1523 the Council of the city maintained a somewhat conservative attitude. But on January 29, 1523, a disputation was held, attended by six hundred prelates, nobles, university doctors and parish priests. In this great ecclesiastical tournament Zwingli was adjudged the victor, and his views those which Zürich must adopt.

Thereupon commenced Zwingli's difficulties. He was a Switzer and a politician, and had great schemes for the strengthening of the Zwinglian Reformation both in Switzerland and Germany. His followers, at least many of the more active among them, bent wholly on a thoroughly scriptural reformation in Church and State, could not understand the sudden halts Zwingli made. To uproot idolatry, reform clerical morals, and obtain more equitable conditions for the classes who had to work—these aims they set before themselves, and vigorously pursued. The last two were at this particular juncture (1535) intimately connected in the popular mind, and explain the frequent attacks on the abbeys and monasteries. For these places, especially the more aristocratic establishments, were glaring object lessons of the iniquity of a few persons living in luxury, idle and dissolute, at the expense of the industrious many. The way these social questions entwined themselves with the reformation of religious doctrines and practices was specially embarrassing to reformers like Zwingli, who, well-aware what storms they had already raised, feared that once again let loose they would engulf the whole effort after religious reformation.

Among those who were most displeased with Zwingli's course were Wilhelm Röubli, preacher at Wytikon; Simon Stumpff, preacher at Höngg; Hans Brötli, curate at Zollikon; Jorg, from "Jacob's House,' a monastic establishment at Chur, better known by his nickname Blaurock[1] ; Felix Manz, and Conrad Grebel; the two last-named being men of learning and citizens of Zürich. The division between Zwingli and those who represented the people's idea of Reform widened more and more. The latter considered their leader unsatisfactory, not only on the question of tithes, but also on that of the Mass; his chief offense, however, lay in his wishing to make the city Council the ruling power in the new church. At a second discussion held in Zürich, October 26–28, 1523, with reference to the Mass, it became clear that the question of the freedom of the Church from State control was the point upon which the struggle with Zwingli would turn. The latter having said that the

---

1. Blaurock: Bluecoat.

Council would decide whether the priests should be instructed with regard to the Mass, Stumpff replied, "You have no power to give the decision in this matter to my lords; the decision is given, the Spirit of God has decided." "Since the October disputation," wrote Conrad Grebel, "it goes badly with the Gospel in Zürich, for Zwingli no longer arranges anything according to the duty of a pastor. The Council look through their fingers at Zwingli, and Zwingli looks through his fingers at the Council." Such was the cynical view at the time. Zwingli maintained the jurisdiction of the Council over everything. The Council turned his proposals into State laws.

While the friends of freedom in religious matters separated more and more from the Zwinglian party, the breach was completed when Stumpff, Grebel, and Manz arrived at the conclusion that the church could only consist of true Christians, and that, following the example of the apostolic communities, such persons ought to separate from the world and gather together as a pure and holy people. Stumpff was soon after exiled, apparently for the strong language about rents and tithes which both he and Röubli had used; but as the latter was hardly punished at all, it seems probable that Stumpff suffered more for his doctrine on the jurisdiction of the Council than for that upon rents and tithes. The little company who united in apostolic fashion with Grebel and Manz were mostly working men. Thus were brought together by a common faith the learned and the unlearned: those who had been brought up in comfort and those who knew what poverty was, and "under the cross their hearts were made one." Both influences worked together—the single-minded faith of those who lived upon the Word of God and had experienced its truth, and the learning of those who were students of the Hebrew and Greek Scriptures, and the result was the reappearance of the forms of primitive Christianity. The apostolic community was restored.

Now side by side were seen in Zürich the germs of two opposing Christendoms: the Church united to the State and subject to its influence and authority, and the Church separated from the world and within its own sphere denying the world's authority. In studying the records of the first Christian community at their meetings held in the house of the

mother of Felix Manz, a spirit of devotion and love arose, giving birth
to a higher form of society, not in the least resembling that of churches
in which the members of the one Body of Christ were encouraged, and
even compelled, to struggle each one to get as much as possible of the
good things of this life for himself, and that to such an extent that this
struggle had become a law of life for the pastors as well as the people. The
New Testament knew nothing, the Brothers said, of interest and usury,
tithes, livings, and prebends; but the Christians it spoke of considered
their earthly goods as belonging to the whole body. Nor did they read of
any among them assuming offices of authority in the world, or using the
sword; their only weapon was suffering, their only means of reforming
offenders, brotherly admonition, and, as a final resort, excommunica-
tion. They could not wholly despair of Zwingli—at least they took pains
to set before him their views. And he answered mildly, "The position
today is not as it was in apostolic times: then it was separation from those
who openly declared against the Gospel; now there are many around us
of whom we have hope, but who, if we separate from them, will become
apostate. There will always be tares among the wheat whatever you do;
therefore, dear brethren, have patience with the weak and foolish ones,
who also belong to Christ."

The leaders of the new community were already in communication
with those who in Holland were treading a similar path, and the writing,
of Strauss,[2] Carlstadt, and Münzer, which came into their hands, led
them to enter into correspondence with the two latter. From Carlstadt
they had a friendly reply; and it is said Münzer made a flying visit into
Switzerland during his journey through South Germany in 1524. Under
date September 5th, 1524, Grebel, with other members of the Zürich
community, sent a letter to their "lieber Bruder Thoman." They are
not wholly satisfied with him; his translation of the mass, and using
it, together with German hymns, as a part of worship, is not good, for

---

2. See the beginning of chapter three for some account of Strauss.

singing is only allowable as a means of teaching or admonishing.[3] Is, they ask, his living supported by rents and tithes? For, if no, he ought to resign it. They learn that he has put up the tables of the Law in the church; there is no authority for this in the New Testament. Through the Word, and relying on Christ, and guided by His rule as given in Matthew 18, he should seek to found a new Church. The Gospel must not be protected by the sword, as they understand he thinks and holds. True Christian believers are sheep for the slaughter, and must, in anguish and need and trouble, suffer persecution and be baptized into death. Thus are they proved, and arrive at eternal peace, not through the slaughter of their earthly, but through the destruction of their spiritual foes. They evidently doubt his knowledge of the true doctrine of baptism, for they tell him "baptism signifies that, through faith and by the blood of Christ, our sins are washed away, that we should die to sin, and walk in newness of life and spirit. All children who do not know the difference between good and evil will be saved through the sufferings of Christ, the new Adam." This epistle is sent to Münzer by Grebel, Castelberger, Manz, Oggenfüsz, Pur, Aberli, and other brethren at Zürich.

From this letter we learn how important the question of baptism had become to the Swiss Brothers, and very soon Röubli was arrested and imprisoned for causing certain parents to neglect, at Zollikon and Wytikon, having their children baptized. He and Brotli were settled at Zollikon as preachers, and to their influence it is ascribed that Zollikon, from 1523–25, became the focus of the Baptist movement in this part of Switzerland. In Zürich, Castelberger, familiarly called Andres Stülzer, or Andres-on-the-crutches, a book-hawker, was the favorite preacher. His doctrine theologically was Zwinglian, but when he spoke of social matters it had the true Anabaptist ring. He often told the crowds that gathered round him, that if pride or contentiousness arose among them he would stop his preachings.

---

3. Notwithstanding this view, Manz and Blaurock wrote hymns, and the Brothers later on had a hymn-book they much prized.

However, these were dangerous times, for through the whole of Central Europe the peoples were waking up and declaring they were free, and would be free. It was alike whether they were Catholic or Reformed, there was everywhere one and the same ardent desire to throw off the yoke. In 1524, in the Helvetic Diet, the complaint was made that the Catholic Cantons were becoming seditious, refusing to pay tithes or taxes, or to fulfil the usual compulsory services; that they claimed community of goods, and showed for authority such contempt that the ruin of the country was imminent. Although the Zürich authorities favored the democratic movement in Germany, it was quite different when its spirit invaded their own domains and tended to break up the order of things on which their power was based. For now a union between the Zwinglian Church and the Canton of Zürich had taken place. Infant baptism had become to the double-headed body what circumcision was to the Hebrew Theocracy, the sign of union with a certain order of things, and a pledge of obedience to its laws and to those appointed to maintain them. And as freedom of choice in the circumcision of children could not be allowed in the Hebrew State without leading to a complete break up of its constitution, so it became with infant baptism where State and Church were really one body. Thus it was that the Zürich authorities came to recognize that denial of infant baptism meant fundamental opposition to the new constitution. And this position manifested itself as each of the articles of the faith of the opponents of infant baptism came into prominence—refusal to take oaths, to use weapons of war, to act as magistrates, or to sanction the punishment of death. It was clear that if these doctrines took root, no Christian State as hitherto understood was possible. It would dissolve, and in its place two societies would be face to face, the Church and the World—not necessarily inimical, but certainly opposed and independent. This controversy was then crucial: if the Brothers were right, the Christendom then existing must cease to be.

The Council determined to try this vital question of infant baptism in a Disputation, which was held on January 17th, 1525. Grebel, Manz, Röubli, Castelberger, Brotli, Blaurock, and Hetzer appeared to defend the view that infants, not being able to exercise faith or understanding, are not in a position to be baptized, and that the rite ought only to be administered to believers who comprehend the meaning of the act. Zwingli replied that infant baptism took the place of circumcision. This, in fact, was an argument he always put forward, and for the reason above stated it probably appeared to him a very strong one. The Council decided that infant baptism must be maintained and opposition to it made illegal. Eight days' grace was to be given, after which anyone neglecting to baptize his children would be banished. Grebel and Manz, as citizens, were held to obedience; while Röubli, Brotli, Hetzer, and Castelberger were ordered to quit the Zürich territory in eight days; the last-named, being ill, was allowed a month's grace. All private meetings were stopped, and on February 1 the arrest was ordered of all persons refusing to baptize children. That under such circumstances the Brethren at Zürich should feel "themselves a little group in presence of a wholly hostile world" is not strange. "In confidence, however, that they possessed the truth, and having in view Christ and His apostles, who through the selfsame road of sorrow went to glory, they cried out, 'It must be won by fighting. O God, grant us intrepid prophets, who, without any additions invented by themselves, shall preach Thine own eternal Word.'"

How the danger affected them the ancient chronicles of the Anabaptists tell us. "And they have desired that they might be nigh one another until they had come out of this anguish. Yea, in their hearts they were pressed, therefore have they begun to bend their knees before the highest God in Heaven, and as one heart in experience crying out in prayer, that He would give them to do His divine will, and to this end would show them His compassion. Neither flesh, nor blood, nor human forwardness has influenced them, for they well knew what they must thereby suffer and endure. After this prayer Blaurock stood up, and, in accordance with the will of God, begged of Conrad Grebel that he would baptize him with a true Christian baptism on his faith and confession; and thereupon, kneeling down, Conrad, in accordance with his prayer, baptized him, no ordained minister at this time having undertaken such work. When this had taken place, the others likewise desired of Blaurock that he would baptize them, which he also has done, and in deep fear of God they have also altogether given themselves to the Lord, one among the converted being appointed as minister of the Gospel; and so they commenced to teach and maintain the faith."[4]

This resuscitation of adult baptism, and of the Lord's Supper as an evening meal, affected those present in such a way that an eyewitness said, "his hair stood on end." It, moreover, so stirred up a sense of union in one Lord that the Brothers and Sisters could not longer bear to call anything they possessed their own, and at Zollikon community of goods was definitely established. From other sources we learn that the Brothers considered baptism as a sign of conversion and reconciliation, through the absolution and remission of sins, and the bread and wine from the table of the Lord as a sign of brotherly love intended for everyone "who believes that in God, by death and bloodshedding, he is redeemed." The bread, they said, is the bread of love, and those who eat it desire to have God always in their hearts and to think about Him, and to show everyone brotherly love. From nearly all comes the testimony that God Himself, the Creator and Savior, has moved them to baptism. They are His servants and obedient subjects, and must not allow any earthly power to hinder them from doing what the Spirit of God commands; and they will only obey the Council so far as its commands are in accordance with the Word of God.

Accordingly they went on preaching and baptizing. Blaurock was called "a second Paul." On Shrove Tuesday, 1525, he preached at Zollikon to about 150 persons, and baptized some. Meeting Aberli in Jakob Hottinger's house, he said, "Brother Heinrich, can you bear witness that the Lord Jesus Christ has suffered for us, and that what is written of Him is true? Aberli gave his word that it was so. Upon which Blaurock, with a handful of water, baptized him, saying, "I baptize thee in the Name of the Father, the Son, and the Holy Ghost."

When the Council heard that baptizing was again going on at Zollikon, they issued a decree that whoever had been baptized since February 8th should be fined a silver mark, and whoever after this presumed to be

---

4. Abschnitt von Aufang de Gemain Gottos in Teutscher Iandt. Die Geschichts-Biicher von Dr. Josef Beck, p. 19.

baptized should be banished, with wife and children. Very soon all the leaders were in prison, and on March 20th, Manz, Blaurock, and Grebel were brought before the Council. Recommitted to prison with their companions, a little congregation of twenty-one persons, they urged those among them who did not feel strength enough to remain faithful to submit to the authorities. Towards the end of the month, one of the prisoners noticing an unclothed shutter in the lobby of the prison, they determined to make their escape, which they did by means of ropes and a swing-bridge. Then, uncertain in what direction to fly, one of them suggested that "they should go to the Red Indians in North America."

This escape soon came to take a legendary form, and the story went about that they had been delivered by an angel and had passed through closed doors. Inhibitions, arrests, examinations, imprisonment, penalties, all these circumstances so agitating for men and women in whom conscience is very strong, were beginning to have their effect. Suddenly a crowd of people, with their loins girded and staves in their hands, are seen marching through Zürich. They stop in the square, and begin to preach moral reformation, conversion to justice, and brotherly love. They denounce the old dragon and his heads, that is, Zwingli and the Council; they prophesy the fall of the city in a short time. "Woe! woe to Zürich," the cry rises through the narrow, densely-populated streets, and its reverberation ceased not until that frightful day, six years later (October 10, 1531), when Zürich learned that its army was completely defeated, Zwingli slain, and the city at the mercy of its Catholic foes. Then, says Bullinger, "there suddenly arose a loud and terrible cry, lamentation and tears, wailing and groaning." And from that day, so disastrous for Zwinglianism, the Catholic restoration began in Switzerland.

2

The persecution which drove the Baptists from Zürich was the means of spreading their ideas. St. Gall, one of the first places to receive the New Baptism, was a city of artisans and traders. The democracy there was rising to power, and in harmony therewith popular gatherings, conducted by laymen, were the form its religious life then took. They were called "Readings," because they consisted in reading and explaining the Scriptures, and took their rise in a visit paid to St. Gall, in 1523, by Dr. Balthasar Hubmaier, of Waldshut, his popularity being such that, after preaching in the churches, he went on to preach in private houses and taverns, and at last at the large hall of the Butchers' Guild. From the beginning of 1524 these "readings" became an institution in St. Gall, and were carried on by Johannes Kessler, a saddler, who had studied at Pâle and Wittenberg. His audiences became so large that he went to the Tailors' Hall. On one occasion, explaining the sixth of Romans, he was questioned by Hochrütiner, a weaver from Zürich, who thereupon set forth the views of the Baptists. Whether it was this, or a general fear of public discussion under the critical circumstances of the times, is not stated, but on September 15th, at the requisition of the Federal Diet, the "Readings" were stopped by the St. Gall Council. On Martinmas Day the people gathered under the lime trees outside the principal church in St. Gall, to hear a new preacher, Wolfgang Schorant, commonly called Uolimann, one of Kessler's helpers. The weather was rough, and the people ran to the various churches to see if they could not open one. After this demonstration the "Readings" were again permitted.

Early in 1525, Grebel was at Hallau, near Schaffhausen, Brotli and Röubli having found there "a great harvest and but few reapers." Meeting Grebel on the way to Schaffhausen in February, 1525, Uolimann, who till then had not accepted adult baptism, was convinced that true baptism must be on a confession of faith, and also that immersion was the right mode. Grebel baptized him in the Rhine. This resuscitation of immersion as the right form of baptism took place at a time when Germany was convulsed by the Peasant War, and France by the defeat and capture of Francis I at Pavia. The lustral waters flowed on through lands where the sky was already lurid and the soil beginning to be soaked in blood.

Uolimann returned to St. Gall, and learning that Kessler was allowed to preach in a church, asked permission to do the same. Being refused, he announced at a great meeting in the Weavers' Hall, on March 18th, that he would teach in the square, the marketplace, the marsh, and elsewhere. Intense feeling prevailed, and the baptized community at St. Gall soon numbered 800 persons. Grebel himself came, and on Palm Sunday led a procession of converts out of St. Gall, and baptized them in the Sitter. Orders were issued against crowds gathering and meetings being held; all citizens were called upon to be armed and to avoid uproar.

When Grebel left St. Gall, Roggenacher, a skinner, and Eberle Polt, a sailor, continued to preach and teach. "The latter," Kessler says, "was a pious, good-hearted man, practiced in the Scriptures, and of agreeable speech." He preached during Eastertide in the Butchers' Hall and on the Berlisberg. Crowds came to be baptized, and, if there was no flowing water at hand, they were baptized in large vessels in the fields, and to each of the baptized a new name was given. The Council got the burgomaster to invite Eberle to his house, and to urge him to go away. He went on the following Friday, and eight days after suffered martyrdom at Schwyz (May 29th).

Meanwhile the other dispersed leaders were working in various directions—some in Switzerland, some in Germany. Manz was arrested at Chur, and sent back to Zürich.

All Baptist teachers from without having been got rid of in St. Gall, Uolimann had to bear the main brunt of the persecution. He was summoned before the Council on the 25th of April for venturing, on his own authority, to baptize and to administer the Lord's Supper. In answering for his deeds he told the Council that the original Christian order was teaching, believing, baptizing; this, he said, lasted until the time of Tertullian and Cyprian, when they began to baptize sick children. Following human reason, infant baptism gradually came to be the rule. Uolimann made an impression, and the usual preliminary to an adverse decree, a disputation, was appointed.

So the learned burgomaster, Dr. von Watt, or Vadian, as in the pedantic style of the time he was called, prepared a defense of infant baptism of so voluminous a character that it is called a book. The Baptists asked for time to consider his arguments. Meanwhile, both Grebel and Zwingli intervened, the latter publishing a work inscribed "To those of St. Gall on Anabaptism and Infant Baptism," in which—after twitting the Baptists for making so much of an external rite, and declaring that their doing so covered other aims—Zwingli affirmed that no one has the right to separate himself from the Church, which, of course, practically meant the Church established by the civil authorities. His chief defense of infant baptism was its analogy with circumcision, and that water baptism being only a sign of allegiance and covenant, and an act with which salvation was not bound up, it might quite well be given to children whose parents belong to the people of God.

Zwingli sent this book with a letter to Vadian on the 21st of May, and on the 30th Grebel tried to minimize its effect on the burgomaster, who was his brother-in-law, by an appeal to his conscience. He supplicated him not to reject the inward teaching of the Spirit of Truth, and to beware of shedding innocent blood; for if a decree of persecution were issued, his would be the responsibility. "Is he not," Grebel asks, "being tempted because thereby he will please the rich and powerful?" "Give up," he says, "the enjoyment of riches, humble yourself, be content with moderation, and withdraw from the bloodthirsty party of Zwingli. Flee from your own wisdom to the divine wisdom, that you may become a simple one in this world but wise toward God."

On June 5th Vadian read his book before the Council, and on the 6th the Baptists replied. But they could hardly have felt it to be more than a protest, since these religious discussions ordered by the authorities had the character of a criminal trial, sure to end in the conviction of the party opposed to the judges. So now, the Baptists were forbidden to baptize, administer the Lord's Supper, or hold separate meetings. They might, however, have reading and prayer in St. Lawrence's Church at certain hours. But persecution was in in the air; refusing to take an oath involved in one case exile, cruel sentences were passed, and men threatened with excision of the tongue.

How the Baptist community at St. Gall appeared to those among their opponents, who were good and disinterested men, we may learn from the testimony of Kessler, who must have known some of them intimately. "Their manners," he says, "appeared pious, godly, and innocent, they avoided all expensive clothing, disdained delicate eating or drinking, went about very humbly clad in a coarse kind of cloth, with broad felt hats, and wore no weapons or ornaments of any kind. They strove more than the Catholics for justification by their works." Another testimony is the fact that, in the very month in which the disputation was held, Hans Denck was living in St. Gall at the house of an Anabaptist. Though not a baptized member of the community, he was certainly an Anabaptist in the highest and most spiritual sense. He wrote a book while staying in St. Gall, with the following characteristic title, "He who really loves the truth can herein examine himself, so that none exalt his faith by reason of some personal experience, but know from whom he should ask and receive wisdom." Its object was to set forth the true method of interpreting the Bible, especially with reference to the opposing views of Luther and of the Roman Church, the former saying it could easily be understood by anyone, the latter that it could only be understood in the light of the teaching of the Councils and Fathers of the Church. In reply to both Denck asserted, with the Zwickau prophets, that it belonged alone to the Holy Spirit, who had written the Bible, and who, in some degree, dwells in every good man, to give the searcher the right interpretation. The title of the book, and its motto, suggest that the fear of God and the love of the truth are essential prerequisites to anyone who would know the mind of the Spirit and the meaning of the Word of God. Therefore, Denck said, we must surrender ourselves both in heart and will to the Master who teaches all the doctors of all the schools, and who alone has the key wherewith all the treasures of wisdom are unlocked.

It is not strange that in this exciting year, and under strain of persecution, some lost their mental balance. In any case we may safely affirm that Thomas Schugger, who thought himself called to cut off his brother's head, was an unfortunate madman, who only needed some exciting cause to make the state of his mind apparent. Other enthusiastic exaggerations there were, as has not unfrequently been the case in religious movements—persons who fell into convulsions, and who described their state as "lost in God," and others who went about the street, crying, "Repent, for the day of the Lord is at hand."

3

Towards the end of April, 1525, the agitation in South Germany was felt in a part of the Canton of Zürich, called the lordship of Grüningen. The cry went up, "We are all free one as another, and are no man's property, and have all one Lord." The movement against feudal burdens was so general that the parsons of several parishes were carried away by it. The monasteries had largely got hold of the land, and the parson of Hinweil advocated a march upon them with drums and fifes, in order to get "the Carnival Cakes." Zwingli's remedy was to get serfage abolished.

Little proof as there is of any attempt on the part of the Baptists to promote the social movement in Grüningen, it is not strange that they were made to suffer for it, since their sympathies were entirely with the People. So bound up was their cause considered to be with the great struggle in Germany, that on the defeat of the Peasants the Zürich Council proceeded to extremities with the Baptists. The usual preliminary disputation was held (November 6–8); Grebel and Manz defended the Baptist view, Zwingli opposing it, while the Abbot of Cappell, Vadian, and Dr. Hoffmeister, of Schaffhausen, kept the lists. Zwingli was declared victorious, and Grebel, Manz, and Blaurock, refusing to submit, were committed to the tower of the Wellenberg, kept on low diet, no visitors allowed them, and no term fixed to their imprisonment. As the rural districts betrayed dissatisfaction at this result, a warning was published about the middle of November in the ten churches of the Grüningen district, and three Baptists, of whom Michael Sattler was one, were imprisoned under the same conditions as their comrades in Zürich.

Among the fugitives in the Grüningen lordship now appeared Dr. Balthasar Hubmaier. He had, as parson of Waldshut, been one with the People in the great rising, and, it is said, was the writer of the "Twelve Articles." In the Easter of this very year he had not only been baptized himself by one of the Zürich exiles, but had himself baptized some three hundred persons. The Austrian Government, whose subject he was, demanded his extradition, but this was refused as neither proper nor customary. However, bringing himself under the new Zürich law against advocating, practicing, or aiding baptism, or harbouring its professors, he was sent to Zürich. Zwingli, finding him more yielding than Grebel and Manz, and not taking their position as regards the magistracy, community of goods, and possibility of a sinless condition; he was treated more gently. But, destitution, illness, and discouragement so preyed upon him that he consented to retract his opinions, and this he did publicly, both at Zürich and at Gossau in Grüningen. After being kept in custody for a time, he was set free and helped to escape the Austrian Government. He reached Constance, where he soon reasserted his convictions, and we shall hear of him again in Moravia.

In March, 1526, Grebel, Manz, and Blaurock, who had been more than three months in prison, were again interrogated, but, persisting in their doctrine, they were treated with still more severity: they were to have no food but bread and water, nothing to lie on, no alteration was to be made in case of illness, they were to be left to die in prison. Their wives and daughters were to be also imprisoned.

On March 7th Zwingli announced to Vadian that the Council had resolved to inflict the penalty of death on the Baptists. A decree now appeared condemning all relapsed Baptists to be drowned. No one was to give a Baptist house or farm, shelter or provision, assistance or harbourage of any kind. Neither the people nor the magistrates in the rural districts would help to carry out this decree. The Baptists, therefore, braved the law, held meetings, and baptized converts. Moreover, the village parsons were so completely one with the people in their opposition to the Government at Zürich, that the officials complained "that five parsons are more regarded by the people than five hundred Government officials," and they "pray their dear lords not to trust the parsons, who are deceitful, lying, and a nuisance."

May 28th, 1526, Zwingli wrote, "All earlier battles have been only child's play. This is revolt, heresy, schism, but not baptism."

On the 5th of January, 1527, the Zürich Council desiring—so they wrote to Augsburg—to terrify, ordered Felix Manz to be drowned. According to the sentence, Manz "was to be given over to the executioner, who was to bind his hands, put him on a ship, lead him to the lower deck, there tie his hands to the naked knees, place a stick between the arms and the legs, and, so bound, throw him into the water, and leave him to die and perish, and so he thereby shall make amends to law and justice." Also "shall his goods fall to my lords."

The same sentence was passed on Blaurock, but as he was not a subject of the Zürich magistracy, it was commuted to public whipping out of Zürich. Stripped to the waist, he was flogged through the city until the blood came, and so expelled through the gate into the lower village. As we never hear any more of Grebel, we may infer that his weakened constitution had already succumbed to the inhuman treatment to which he was subjected. Manz, who was strengthened by his mother and brother, left an exhortation to the Brothers which, while evidently the composition of an ardent believer in Christ, and of one who is sure that nothing avails with God but love, glows with resentment against those who professed to be shepherds and teachers, but acted as Cain, who slew his brother.

These cruelties were repeated in other parts of Switzerland. Under the government of Bâle certain Baptist prisoners, among them a young girl of seventeen years of age, were immersed in a stream three times in one day, and one was drowned. Ludwig Hetzer, who with Denck translated the Prophets, was beheaded at Constance, February 4th, 1529. "A more glorious and manful death," says an eyewitness, "was never seen in Constance." Another wrote, "As he finished his address to the bystanders he looked to heaven with beaming eyes. The people, touched and filled with compassion, wept."

Of Michael Sattler's glorious martyrdom we shall speak further on; with him died Matthias Kursner and Gabriel Giger, both of St. Gall. Giger was the first who became an Anabaptist in St. Gall. He felt himself moved to go to Zürich and to be baptized by Grebel Uolimann and Blaurock, who had both done so much for the cause in Switzerland, were burnt to death in the Tyrol.

The Zürich authorities, unable to affect the rural districts, called a Diet of the cities and cantons with whom they were in confederacy with a view to extirpating Anabaptism. To this Diet (1527) came deputies from the lordship of Grüningen, who set forth the views of the people, concluding, "We demand therefore that you let us abide by the truth;

but if that may not be, we are ready to suffer for the truth through the grace and power of God given us." The Zürich authorities were evidently supported by the general opinion of the Diet, for during the next year they brought two of the Grüningen prisoners, Jakob Falk and Heini Reimann, to Zürich, and on the 5th of September drowned them in the middle of the river.

In the lowlands of the canton there were the same complaints of fugitives from Waldshut, and stronger ones of absence from church, of crowds collecting together, of sympathy on the part of officials or their relatives, of refusal to take an oath, of attacks on prisons, of secret preaching in woods and at midnight. On the other hand, there was no sympathy, as in the highlands, between parsons and people, and the records of the first synod of Zürich—Easter, 1528—show the reason why. The parsons of the Zürich lowlands were chargeable with gross immorality, and a historian, far from friendly to the Anabaptists, admits that the reformation of the morals of the Zwinglian clergy must be put to the credit of the Baptist movement in the lowlands. After the revelations made at the first synod of the Zürich clergy, Zwingli seems to have fought the Baptist faith in the canton by the double process of persecuting those who held it, and by efforts to elevate the moral character of those who were to represent the established religion. The persecution was not so ruthless as in Catholic countries, but its prolonged torture was, perhaps, more difficult to bear. A number of Baptists were left a year and fifteen weeks in prison, one of whom was swollen from dropsy, probably the effect of the miserably low diet on which they seem to have kept their Baptist prisoners. The leader in the lowland district, Konrad Winkler, was put to death by drowning, January 20th, 1530.

In other districts the means were the same—persistent hard dealing with the Baptists and mandates in support of public morality. Finding the opposition failing, a final blow was struck in the lowlands by whole-sale arrests. In December, 1529, and during the early part of 1530, quite a host of Baptists are on their trial, in several cases entire families, the object being to crush out the noxious plant of Anabaptism by destroying all its seed vessels. Very little new comes out of the examinations. The old points are emphasized.

"It is," said the accused, "unchristian to shed the blood even of a murderer: such people must be shut up and their conversion sought. Anything beyond simple affirmation is contrary to the law of Christ. We possess nothing of ourselves; all has been purchased. To sum up: simple, poor people are precluded from a right understanding of the Scriptures, for they are not truly and completely interpreted."

The policy of "thorough" was now put in force. Incarcerated Baptists were simply kept in prison until they yielded. Complete silence characterized the second half of the year 1530, and Zwingli was free to act against the Baptists abroad, and to work on his great scheme of combining the Protestant Cantons into a union for religious freedom, together with Strassburg and the Suabian cities. It is said that he dreamed of nothing less than of founding an Evangelical Empire on the ruins of the Roman Empire.

A year hardly passed away before Zwingli, who was intellectually head and shoulders above any of his compatriots, met the fate of one of whom this was true physically. Like King Saul, Zwingli suddenly came to a tragically miserable end.

Titles of Works Consulted

- Egli, E.: *Die Zürcher Wiedertäufer.*

- Egli, E.: *Die St. Galler Wiedertäufer.*

- Cornelius: *Geschichte des Münsterischen Aufruhrs, Bl. 2.*

- Beck, J.: *Geschichtsbücher der Wiedertäufer.*

- Van Braght: *Het Bloedig Tooneel of Martelaers Spiegel der Doopsgezinde.*

- Underhill, E. B.: *Martyrology of the Churches of Christ, commonly called Baptists* (Translated from the former work).

- Burrage, H. S.: *History of the Anabaptists in Switzerland.*

3

Anabaptism in the Tyrol and Moravia

1

The spirit of reform which, early in the sixteenth century, appeared in all parts of the German Empire, reached the Tyrol by means of the many wandering adventurous people, who, for objects religious or secular, dared to face the great difficulties of travelling in those days. Among these were ardent champions of the new teaching, who brought with them books and pamphlets in its explanation or defense. As early as 1521 some had begun publicly to preach its Gospel in the Tyrol. In that year Dr. Jakob Strauss, a monk, preached in the open air to the miners of Schwaz district, and at Hall, where both in the churches and public places he gathered great crowds. Cited to Brixen to answer for his attacks on the clergy, the people of Hall would not allow his arrest, and the bishop was informed that his preaching was evangelical. However, the Council was ordered by the Government at Innsbruck to send Strauss away privately, as he was "a dangerous heretic and a rebel." He accordingly left for Saxony in May, 1522, to the sorrow and indignation of the people, who showed him many marks of affection. After a time, he was heard of at Eisenach, where, from a pamphlet he published in 1524, it is clear that his sentiments and tone of mind were those of the early Anabaptists: an ardent love for "the Common Man," and a burning sense of the wrongs he had endured and was enduring. The Swiss Baptists, as already stated, read his writings, and this attraction to Strauss, which they shared in common with the Tyrolese, is proof that both were influenced by the same spirit.

In this early stage of the Reformation in the Tyrol, three things are noticeable: (1) the monasteries are mostly the sources from which the preachers come; (2) the laity are generally favorable to the Reformation, as proved by the action of the subordinate authorities in town and country; (3) the persons most intent on preserving the old order are the ruling princes, the Archduke Ferdinand, whose title changes after a time into "King," and his brother, the Emperor Charles V.

To the help of the reforming clerics came a number of laymen, metal-workers, and students. The focus of the movement was the brotherhood formed in the midst of the large mining population at Schwaz. The silver mines in that neighborhood, now exhausted, were a kind of Mexico or Peru to the Austrian Court at Vienna, for it drew from them no less a sum than 300,000 florins annually. The mines were farmed by the great Augsburg bankers, the Fuggers, who extracted from them for their own share a yearly yield of 200,000 florins. These facts let a flood of light on the zeal the Archduke Ferdinand personally displayed against the very idea of reform in the Tyrol. His wider field of observation, together with his deeper personal interest, made him clear-sighted beyond even the experienced officials at Innsbruck—to say nothing of the subordinate authorities all over the Tyrol, who often felt more with the people than with the prince, and could not, or would not, see the peril it was to things as they were for men to go about preaching of sin and judgment to come. It was the impression these preachers gave—that justice and truth, heaven and hell, God and eternal judgment were realities; that Christ was really a redeemer and a king, so that His laws were a thousand times more binding than any imperial mandates; that the Church He had founded ought to be a holy community, a true fellowship, to the existence of which liberty, equality, and fraternity were necessary conditions—it was the sense of the reality of these things which their preaching created, which affected, as the blast of trumpets that brought down the walls of Jericho, the existing order of things in Church and State.

In 1525, the great Peasant Insurrection appeared as likely to be successful in the Tyrol as in other parts of the Empire. Ferdinand, writing to the commander of the mercenaries he had collected to put the peasants down, said, "Sad reports follow each other rapidly, the peasants on all sides are so threatening that we do not pass a single day in safety; we are expecting every day to be surprised at Innsbruck."

The peasants met in the plain of Mühlen on the Eisack and marched on Brixen, Whitsun night, 1525. They attacked the bishop's palace and drove out the episcopal council. The inhabitants of Brixen made common cause with the peasants and, joining together, they set out for the abbey of Neustift, which they wrecked. Thereon followed attacks everywhere throughout the Tyrol on the higher and wealthier clergy. The leader of the insurgents, Michael Geismayr, proposed to reorganize the Tyrol on the following plan.

The pure Word of God to be preached fully and faithfully. All books treating the subject in a sophistical, pettifogging manner to be burnt. In the city chosen as the seat of the Government, a university to be established where the pure Word of God should be exclusively taught. Three wise men chosen from the teachers, expert in the Scriptures (from which alone the justice of God can be learned) to sit in the Council of the Regency to decide all things according to the Divine law, governing the Christian people according to equity.

All images, statues, field oratories to be destroyed, and the mass abolished. Ecclesiastical plate and jewelry to be applied to ordinary uses. Monasteries to be turned into hospitals and charitable institutions. A pastor to be settled in each parish, who will preach the Gospel according to St. Paul. Any surplus in the tithes for his support to go to the poor, not only to supply them with food but also clothing. If that proves insufficient, the poor should become a charge on the revenue.

All social arrangements to be founded on human freedom and equality. All privileges to be abolished as contrary to the word of God and justice. No one having a right to any advantage refused to another. Fortifications, castles, and fortresses were to be razed. Henceforth, there would be no cities, only villages. Taxes were to be levied by each district according to its needs, and in the way each district deems suitable. All customs houses were to be abolished, imports to be free, and exports alone to pay duty. Foundries and mines owned by nobles, foreign merchants, or trading companies were to be confiscated. A superintendent would be appointed to manage them in the general interest. A new and good coinage would be struck, and the old and all foreign money would be withdrawn from circulation.

In the future, no one would be allowed to trade at pleasure, and so no one would be tempted to load his conscience with the sin of usury. To prevent difficulties and to enable goods to be sold at a fair price, a special city, Trieste, for example, would be selected as the location where all necessary commerce could take place. Every trade would find a place there, and the produce of the land would be brought there. Stores would be opened in certain localities where all necessary items would be sold at cost price. The managers and general superintendent would be allowed no profit, but would be paid fixed salaries.

A government elected by the people and sitting at Brixen would watch over the interests of the entire community. Each commune would elect its own judge and eight jurors, and justice would be administered every Monday. No suit would be adjourned beyond a fortnight, and judges, jurors, law writers, barristers, and all necessary attendants would accept nothing beyond their fixed salaries. Although this constitution never got beyond a mere sketch, it clearly shows what the Tyrolese leaders aimed at, and is another light on the popular idea of the Reformation, of which Anabaptism was the religious side.

But the people of the Tyrol were defeated; 9,000 were slain, the leader being beheaded or hanged. The constitution they planned, with its provision for the unhampered preaching of the Gospel in every place, according to the doctrine of St. Paul, is in itself a proof of the widespread influence of Lutheran teaching in the Tyrol. When, therefore, Luther immediately after the defeat of the Thuringian peasants, made his passionate utterance against them and generally exhibited himself as the opponent of the popular cause, he lost vast portions of the lands conquered for the Gospel as he understood it, among others the Tyrol, which fell away from Lutheranism and welcomed a form of faith more in harmony with its political and social aspirations. Already during the insurrection of 1525 or immediately after, there were some Baptists in the Tyrol, for at some time prior to the summer of 1526 Caspar Ferber, from the Innthal, helped to form the Baptist community at Augsburg.

2

In 1527, the Tyrolean Baptists were reinforced by immigrants from Switzerland and other places. And about the same time, a native apostle appeared—Wolfgang, a cowherd from the Sarnthal. At his arrest, the greater part of the miners of Clausen rallied round him. His preachings were also approved by certain priests, and by some who are called "distinguished persons," perhaps nobles, as Anton von Wolkenstein and Helene von Freiburg, the lady of Münichau, both of whom made their houses asylums for the persecuted Baptists. Copies of a mandate against Anabaptism, published in November 1527, were disseminated in the Tyrol in order that "the Common Man" should not in future be excused on the ground of want of knowledge. The authorities sent out orders to torture any who were arrested as Anabaptists, that by means of the information extracted the sect might be utterly destroyed. Schwaz, the miners' town, was found to be a center, and the prisons in the Castle of Freundsberg were so full that they had to take prisoners elsewhere. The overseer of the mines, Stephan Leder, was among those arrested; also a Baptist teacher, Hans Schlaffer. At Sterzing, another mining center, there were also Baptist conventicles.

The degree to which the Baptists were watched is seen in the following police information concerning four Baptists from Clausen, who were going from place to place, "One, named Mayerhofer, has a long brown beard and wears a grey soldier's coat; a companion, tall and pale, wears a long black coat with trimmings; a third is shorter; a fourth, thin, and of a ruddy complexion, who is known as a cutler."

About this time the arrest took place at Rattenberg of the first Baptist bishop in Upper Austria, Leonard Schiemer, or Schoener. Ferdinand of Austria, now King of Bohemia, made Schiemer's so-called confession a pretext for warning the landowners of the Tyrol that "the preaching of the new baptism can lead to no other result than all sorts of revolts, insurrections, and mutinies of the common man against the upper and hereditary class. An inevitable necessity demands that such dangerous fire should be extinguished, for, if it should get the upper hand, no council would be able to stop it."

Ferdinand, however, did not find the local magistrates very willing to carry out his policy of "extinction." The magistrate of Rattenberg, where Schiemer was imprisoned, refused to lie in wait for Baptists, as this was not his office. He allowed the prisoner pens, ink, and paper, thus enabling Schiemer to leave some graphic touches of the intensity of the persecution. "The doctrine of God (he wrote) is forbidden. It is called heresy, a seducing thing, seditious teaching. Therefore the edict and mandate must go out to every corner of the land. Hither gallops the flying post, thither runs the constable; here comes the magistrate, there the governor; here is a scaffold, there is the hangman, and in every house there is an informer. 'I do not do it willingly,' says the latter, 'but I must take care I do not get into disgrace with the Prince.'"

In a second epistle we meet with this characteristic message, "And if Jorg Zaunried (Zaunring) should come to you, I will, so far as he will follow me, that he should be married. To me in the valley of lamentation the Lord commands, let them, if they will, be married. What God calls good, let not man call evil. Who holds the married state for sin is a teacher of Antichrist." It was determined to make Schiemer's trial "brave and imposing"—at least, such is the reason given why the magistrate was to associate with himself in the judgment-seat twenty councilors from various places; probably, however, it was to prevent the judge himself from succumbing to popular opinion in his district.

Leonard Schiemer was beheaded on the 14th of January, 1528, at Rattenberg. This execution was followed by the execution of seventy others who also sealed their testimony with their blood in the same place. In the same year, Hans Schlaffer and Leonard Fryk were executed. Schlaffer, under torture, declared that their faith, actions, and baptism rested on the commandment to "Go ye into all the world, and preach the Gospel to every creature. He that believeth and is baptized shall be saved." He said that their only aim was to renounce the blasphemous living of the world and that he gave up being a priest for conscience's sake. However, he acknowledged that he believed God had appointed him to be a prophet.

Kitzbühel was a city of refuge for the Baptists, and in order to terrorize them, some who had recanted were brought into the square and taunted by the magistrates, "Ah! how bravely do your shepherds and teachers now lay down their lives for you." At this taunt, one of the Baptist teachers, Thomas Harman, sprang from the crowd and cried out, "That which I have taught you is the truth, and I witness it with my blood." He was burnt to death. Many others also suffered at Kitzbühel.

In the Zillertal, the Baptists were numerous, and they were especially strong among the miners at Rattenberg. It was reported that a little book was to be published, in which Anabaptism would be presented in pictures for those who could not read.

The punishment for the "seducing sect" was made even more severe. Those who refused to abjure were to be burnt alive, with beheading reserved only for those who repented after condemnation. In any case, property was forfeited. No repentance would avail baptizers or those who fell away a second time to the Baptists. Houses where the Lord's Supper had been celebrated were to be pulled down. "I have seen with my own eyes," wrote Conrad Braun, assessor to the Imperial Chamber, "that nothing has been able to bring back the Anabaptists from their errors or to decide them to abjure. The hardest imprisonment, hunger, fire, water, the sword, all sorts of frightful executions have not been able to shake them. I have seen young people, men, women, go to the stake, singing, filled with joy, and I can say that in the course of my whole life nothing has moved me more."

Public opinion was so much against this bloodshed that the local authorities were evidently in a difficult position and perpetually offended the Government by their lack of zeal. Governors were even accused of aiding and abetting the Baptists. However, where the Government had docile instruments, the persecution was thorough.

At Sterzing, Hall, and Kitzbühel, so many people united themselves with the Baptists that the prisons were no sooner emptied than they were filled again. The people were so ardent in their desire for martyrdom that "the blood-red rose to pluck, for which the true heart fondly yearned." Their ardour was not lessened by the degrading form of recantation enforced. Bareheaded and barefooted, those who recanted had to walk in procession on two Sundays before the parish priest and sign an abjuration.

"I believe," says Kirchmair, "that in the Tyrol and Gorizia alone a thousand persons have been burnt alive, beheaded, or drowned."[1]

However, the extermination of the Baptists did not proceed fast enough for King Ferdinand, and it was suggested that trusty persons should be employed who would *let themselves be baptized*, and so easily come to know all. One could give such people secretly fifty[2] to sixty guilders. Spies were found willing to commit this blasphemous, traitorous act for forty Rhenish guilders. In spite of all, the movement spread to such an extent that, on one side of the Brenner alone, fifty places are mentioned where, in the course of the year 1529, Baptists were known to be. Notwithstanding the aid of the military in tracking out meetings in the woods and mining galleries, it seldom happened that "the whole nest" was taken. Popular sympathy showed itself in repeated protests by the jurors against the perpetual pouring out of blood, and frequently they refused to share the responsibility.

The burning piles everywhere darkened the sky. The jails were filled with miserable prisoners, the country was full of forsaken houses and hungry, weeping children, and there was not a ray of hope that the trouble would come to an end. Then the Tyrolese Baptists called to mind that God had gathered a people in Moravia, and they determined to send Jakob Huter and Sigismund Schützinger to inquire about these people. They arrived in Moravia during the autumn of 1529, and on their return reported that they had conferred with the elder of the community, Jakob Wiedermann, and had united together with him in peace and oneness of spirit. The Tyrolese were encouraged, and all who felt that they had no longer place or position in their own land were dismissed to the community at Austerlitz, in Moravia.

---

1. Janssen, Vol. III, p. 103. Kirchmair wrote a book on the remarkable occurrences of his time, 1519–1539. He was a Roman Catholic.

2. Loserth, p. 50.

The most careful watching of bypaths and questioning of every stranger, the payment of informers to creep about under disguise of friendship, and the carrying on of trials with closed doors—all had failed, and the Government at Innsbruck, reporting to King Ferdinand, deplore the non-success of their prosecutions. More than 700 men and women had been executed, and yet these people are not frightened. The only remedy is persistence in the executions, and that with much greater assiduity. The date of this report is February 9th, 1530.

Nothing was more abhorrent to the persecuted Baptists than the effort to turn them into informers. In their writings, the informer is branded. The severest torture could not extract from the brothers and sisters the secret of Jakob Huter's temporary abode as, defying all dangers, he indefatigably went from valley to valley, making the faithful happy with the forbidden Word of God.

If the doctrine of the Anabaptists did not actually spring from that of the Hussites, it came from the same source—the soul of the poor of Christendom in all ages. And it ended in the same way: the great majority taking the sword, the few only convinced that the true Christian way was non-resistance to evil.

Among the successors of Huss, Peter of Chilcicky[3] was in 1457 leader of this smaller section. He was opposed to all dogma, all power, all war. Love to God was the essential idea in his teaching. The Truth must not be defended by the sword; the Gospel can only conquer by love. The Church should free itself from all power, all wealth, every tie that binds it to the earth. Power was of pagan origin, and no Christian man could accept it. Equality ought so to prevail among Christians as to render impossible among them royalty, public functions, titles, distinctions. The people ought not to pay taxes, tributes, dues or interest, or perform forced labor. The Christian cannot demand justice of the royal courts or seek protection. To support outrages with resignation, to suffer

---

3. The author of the Sit'viry (the Net of the Faith) a poor man, with a name unknown to "the wise and prudent," but whose influence has never ceased to affect Christendom, and never will cease.

persecution, such is the duty of every Christian man. Peter's writings drew around him many disciples, and 1457 is the date given when, calling themselves Brethren of the Law of Christ, or the United Brethren, they definitely separated from the militant Hussites. They soon spread into Moravia, Silesia, Brandenburg, and Poland. Their apostles travelled without any apparent means; their poverty, obscurity, democratic sympathies gave them easy access to the heart of "the Common Man." Under the influence of the general movement for reform at the opening of the sixteenth century these communities came into prominence. Communications passed between them and Luther. They seem to have been regarded by the persecuted in Germany and elsewhere as harbor lights indicating a place of refuge. To them the Tyrolese now turned in their distress.

Persecution was active wherever the Austrian authorities had power, and whenever they were not too much occupied by the Turks to use it. At Linz, in Austria, seventy-three persons suffered death by fire, water, or the sword. The story seems to come from these parts of Europe that when the people saw a pillar of smoke ascending to the sky, then they believed that the soul of a Baptist was passing to Heaven. So, too, they believed that the heart of a Baptist could not be burnt, however the fire might destroy everything else. At the execution of Hans Blietle, a Moravian bishop, it is said that the smoke of his burning rose directly upwards over him, and that his soul ascended therein. Some said that they saw a beautiful white dove hover in the fire and fly above him to heaven. To prevent the impression these public executions produced the authorities at times put the martyrs privately to death. Thus, when those who were anxiously on the watch heard in the stillness of the night a muffled noise in the waters of the Etsch or the Danube, they knew that a poor Baptist, without the consolation of the tearful sympathetic crowd, had passed through the darkest hour of his trial. "The blood of the Poor," as Cornelius says "flowed as water."[4]

---

4. Münsterischen Aufruhrs, B. II., p. 58

3

While persecution raged in great part of the Austrian dominions, Moravia[5] became a sanctuary or asylum for the persecuted fugitives from Switzerland, Germany, and the Tyrol. Estates were vast and labor scarce; the landlords were glad, therefore, to welcome hard-working people. But when in 1526 Moravia fell under the rule of the House of Austria, it ceased to be a safe retreat. King Ferdinand's position, however, was not at first so secure that he could afford to alienate any of the Moravian nobles. One of these, the lord of Liechtenstein, received Balthasar Hubmaier at Nikolsburg. In this "Emmaus," as the fugitive called it, he not only won Liechtenstein but also two preachers to his views; and the whole community at Nikolsburg, lord, preachers, and people, appear to have been baptized. About 1527 the leaders of this and possibly of other communities held an important meeting on the subject of war and the war tax. It was no academic discussion, for affairs were such that the Turks might at any time be expected to invade the domains of the new King of Bohemia. Hans Hut[6] and Jakob Wiedermann held that Christians could neither take part in war nor pay the war tax, and the former got into such trouble with the lord of Liechtenstein, who was of the opposite opinion, that he was imprisoned in the castle. The two parties came to be called the "Schwertler" or "Sworders," and the "Stabler" or "Staffers." Hubmaier led the "Schwertler," Wiedermann the "Stabler." But a more important point of difference was the degree of importance to be attached to the idea of "the Community." To the "Stabler," a thoroughly strict communism with relation to property was an essential article of their creed. The Stabler accordingly determined to leave Nikolsburg. Liechtenstein led them to the boundaries of his

---

5. Moravia was incorporated into Bohemia in 1029 and went with that kingdom, as well as the rest of the possessions of Louis II of Hungary, to Ferdinand of Austria at the date mentioned in the text.

6. For more particulars concerning Hans Hut see pp. 67–69 (chapter 4, section 3).

domain, drank a parting glass with them, and so they went on their way to Austerlitz. Here their coming was so far welcomed that wagons were sent to help them on their journey, and permission was given to them to build houses in the "Hafenmarkt." The owners of Austerlitz knew the value of honest labor.

In 1527, probably towards the close of that year, Hubmaier and Liechtenstein were summoned to Vienna, the former being imprisoned with his wife in the castle of Greifenstein. A few months later, the Moravian communities learned that on March 10, 1528, Hubmaier was burnt in Vienna and that eight days after his wife was drowned in the Danube. A somewhat severe persecution followed, but though the Austrian Government kept its eye on the Baptists, it was during the next year in such distress that from April to October, the Baptists had rest. This was due immediately to the Turks, who were not only in Hungary, but before Vienna. Ferdinand's capital was circled with flames, and the coming and going of the Turks through his territories were marked by lines of fire.

Owing apparently to a lack of organization, the Baptists at Austerlitz were in a state of disagreement, so that when the Swiss Roubli arrived there as a refugee, he found two parties. After a time, he led a section, mostly Tyrolese, Swabians, and Rhinelanders, to Auspitz, where the abbess of King's Cloister in Brunn allowed them to settle. To put an end to these discords, Huter and Schützinger came in the autumn of 1529 to Moravia. They blamed the Austerlitz community for separating from the innocent, for permitting private property and marriages with unbelievers. Such was the view of Huter and the stricter Baptists on private property that Roubli himself was withdrawn from on account of his keeping back money for unforeseen events, and his charge was given to Zaunring. The communities at Austerlitz and Auspitz deposed all their pastors, even Zaunring, who had been Huter's companion and Schiemer's friend. Schützinger now came and took charge of the Austerlitz community, and a certain unity seemed to prevail among the various sections of Anabaptists in Moravia.

In the summer of 1533, the persecution in the Tyrol becoming too great for endurance, Huter was sent again to Moravia to prepare the way for a more complete exodus of the Tyrolese Baptists. The communities in Moravia became so numerous between 1526-1536 that there were "households" in eighty-six different places. These households consisted of families and single persons who lived in community in one dwelling. Some dwellings contained 400 to 500, and even 600 persons; one numbered 2,000. How far these households formed distinct communities, and to what extent the various communities were one society, is not clear. But it is certain that there were differences among them sufficient to make it very difficult for them to keep in unity. The communities led by Gabriel Ascherham at Rossitz and by Philip Plener at Auspitz may have held anti-Trinitarian views, as did their leaders.[7] But the charge made against them by Huter and his brethren was that they were lukewarm on the community principle. And no doubt it was to counteract their tendency to individualism in faith and action that Huter worked so assiduously to maintain the communistic idea.

Under the system which he is mainly credited with developing, there was over each household one who took the general superintendence, who was called the householder. With him were a number of persons called ministers of the necessities. Each household had a common kitchen, a common bakehouse, a common brewhouse, a common schoolhouse, a common room for childbirth, another for mothers with young infants, and a common nursery in which community sisters looked after the children. Other sisters attended to the sick. The old people were cared for with even more pains and attention than the young, who were strictly kept from the world, no mixed marriages being allowed. No idler was permitted in the community.

The meals were common, but each family had its own rooms. In the morning, after silent prayer, they all went to work, some in the fields, others in the workshops. They put their wages into a common box, which was under the care of a treasurer. Frugal living and assiduous working brought wealth. The communities came to have houses and lands, machinery and shops. But their property was not used simply

---

7. J. Loserth: Der Communismus der Mährischen Wiedertäufer (p. 7).

for the benefit of the particular community that had earned it, but for
the whole body of baptized believers. Vice was practically unknown,
and if any evils did arise, the only punishments resorted to were public
reproof, suspension from the communion of the Lord's Supper, and,
finally, exclusion from the community.

The security enjoyed in Moravia attracted many immigrants from
Silesia, the Palatinate, and the Tyrol. It is said that the Moravian communities numbered at this time 70,000 persons.[8] They refused no one on
account of poverty if he gave evidence of being born again. Their emissaries went in all directions, saying, "What will you do" they said, "when
you become old, when you lie on your bed in a lingering illness, when
famine, bad times, or some misfortune overtakes you? Poor wretches are
we both in summer and winter. Is it not better to gather up all the scraps
we possess and give them over to a holy society, which henceforth will
provide us with food and clothing? Do you desire a quiet life, here you
will find it. Do you care for your children and your children's children,
then come on to Moravia."[9]

The members of the community met twice a year at the Lord's Table
with a recollectedness that called forth the admiration of their foes. The
Supper was to them a pledge of brotherly love, a consolation to mourn-
ers, and a strengthening for bonds, imprisonment, and martyrdom. The
cup they all drank from symbolized the bearing of the sorrows of the
world, through which they were primarily educated for Heaven. After
the festival, they sent forth apostles to all parts, even as far as the Rhine.

4

The exodus from the Tyrol left behind it the poorer and feebler members
of the flock. Meetings continued to be held at night in the shafts of
worked-out mines, or among the smelting houses. There were gatherings

---

8. Geschichte der Wiedertäufer, Hast., p. 212.

9. Hast., p. 199.

of as many as fifty to sixty persons in the summer of 1531, but they appeared and disappeared as rapidly as the moon on a cloudy, wind-driven night. The Government now determined to dragoon the country, and on the 6th of February, 1532, a mandate went out commanding "that no shelter be given by anyone to Anabaptists, not so much as the smallest creeping hole, because these people are like murderers, and are enemies of the country, whom everyone ought to be willing to knock down and take to prison." Three weeks later, another mandate styles them "these wicked and pernicious people." The authorities at various places are to watch the water traffic and especially to look out for Jakob Huter, who is described as clothed in a black, coarse, woolen coat with arms, a pleated doublet, white hose, a black hat, and carrying a pickaxe on his arm. He is said to have passed the rapids of the Inn, going down the stream on a voyage towards Austria. On the 12th of May, 1532, another mandate was directed against those who house and harbor this sect, "more and more given up to a life in every way scandalous and shocking." Imprisonment, torture, and finally death will be the result to those who persist in helping Anabaptists, even if they themselves are not Anabaptists.

The Government reports from time to time give glimpses of Huter and the movement generally. Thus Huter has been preaching to eighty or ninety persons near some water in a wood, not one being arrested. At one place, he has been baptizing, and again at another. He is reported to move about for the most part at nighttime and to be supported by peasants who are "going to ruin," and especially by Hans, a peasant who lives, such is the minuteness of the description, in the "last house in Sclunyren."

At executions, the Government insisted that the whole sentence should be read, with all its horrifying details, and the people kept in order by such words as "Stand back!" "Give way!" "What are you doing there?"

The executioner's work went on bravely at Sterzing, where a roving regiment scoured the country like a pack of bloodhounds. Still, the faithful abounded everywhere. In a house at Vilnoss, shortly before Candlemas, 1533, a Communion was held at which seventy persons out of the Pusterthal were present.

Not only do we read of individual executions, but of large numbers being executed together. In June, a great meeting was held in Guffidaun to explain how fugitives could reach Moravia. Eighteen were arrested and eleven executed. On 14th July, many men and women were executed at Brixen, driven in by the bloodhound regiment. "With shocked heart and weeping eyes," says Huter, in a letter from Moravia, "I have read how very great and severe is the persecution."

Further cruelties were added; the prisoners were treated, as those of Giant Despair, with low diet and floggings. The reward for important captures ran as high as 100 guilders, and again the chief officials and magistrates are commanded to appoint certain persons to get themselves baptized in order to betray the meetings.

In June 1533, we get a glimpse of a party in flight to Moravia, so large that they had twenty-five children amongst them. They moved secretly along through bypaths, and mostly at nighttime, reaching Auspitz with the loss of four stragglers. As a rule, parties did not number more than ten to fifteen. Directions were given to each person regarding places and contacts. Unfortunately, the government, in arresting a fugitive, obtained possession of the itinerary.

The tyranny was most intense in 1533. The people clearly became desperate, no longer appearing to care about gentleness or exculpatory statements to appease their tyrants. Margaret Puchl in May 1533, probably under torture, said she held the Church as a heap of stones, the Mass as a horror and a stench before God. Gertrude Piezin in July 1533 declared that she would not recant, desired no pardon, and would rather die with God's help. After such merciless persecution, the authorities were astonished by such unwavering courage and attributed it to diabolism. Consequently, the Governor of Guffidaun was ordered to attempt pouring holy water into the Anabaptists' drinks and sprinkling their food with consecrated salt.

5

The refugees from the Tyrol, coming directly from the midst of the fires of persecution, considered the Brothers in Moravia wanting in earnestness and austerity. Schutzinger, Huter's former companion, failed to rise to their standard of ministerial duty, and they accordingly welcomed as "a grace and compassion of God" the coming of Huter himself to set things in order. Not so the leaders in the various communities. Schützinger announced that he would neither surrender his office nor share it with Huter. Gabriel Ascherham and Philip Plener supported him, and at the meetings all the speakers appeared to be against Huter. However Huter felt it his mission to bring the community up to the true ideal as he conceived it, and he not only set it before them by preaching, but instituted an inquiry into the faithfulness of Schützinger and his wife on the question of private property. A visit to their rooms not only revealed a hoard, but Schützinger confessed to a still larger one hidden in the roof. The visitors were startled, for they did not expect the pastor himself would have been guilty of such a thing. When the matter was brought before the Brothers and Sisters they were affected to tears. Schlitzinger appealed for grace and compassion, but he and his wife were both excommunicated. After a whole week spent in prayer, the Community informed Gabriel that God had sent them Huter, binding him to them in great love, that he might be their bishop and pastor. Being assembled together a fortnight later, Philip and Gabriel appeared, accompanied by two others, apparently leaders, Blasius and Peter Huter. They had come to inquire about the recent excommunications; they were not satisfied, and their visit ended "in high words and flat contradiction." Finally, standing up with the rest of his companions, Gabriel said, "Dear Community, we have nothing against you, but only against your minister. We counsel you, elect some men among yourselves who shall judge in this matter." Upon which, no answer being given, they went forth. In the sequel, the two sections seem to have excommunicated one another. The "Huterischen" shut out Gabriel and Philip with the communities they led from "the Community of God"—the "Philippischen" refused to eat or even work with those who followed Huter.

Another point upon which Huter was solicitous was that Brothers and Sisters, who had attained a marriageable age, should enter into wedlock. He felt the difficulty, "everyone knowing how to mate themselves best, and besides he feared, in speaking the truth on the subject, that he might say too little or too much." Whether it was due to him, or whether it was an earlier arrangement, it came to be the special concern of the community to see each man and each woman rightly married. The wishes of each were in the first place consulted, but other considerations also had weight with the pastors and elders who finally decided the marriage. This arrangement it would seem proved satisfactory.

In a royal edict for the levy of a land tax in Moravia, in the spring of 1535, King Ferdinand said, "It is a well-known fact that in the Netherlands the Anabaptists, committed to prison and held in subjection, have in the sequel begun to rebel against authority. Accordingly, neither Lutherans nor Zwinglians, nor, in fine, any sect will suffer among them these heretics; it is, therefore, the will and intention of His Majesty not to suffer them any more in Moravia." And to Ferdinand's satisfaction, the Moravian Diet agreed with him that the Anabaptists should be driven out of the country.

The landlords on whose estates they had formed settlements now ordered them to quit. The abbess of King's Cloister, in Brunn, who had allowed them to establish themselves at Auspitz and Steurowitz, and the marshal Johann vou Lipa, on whose estates the "Huterischen" were settled, both requested the Brothers and Sisters to quit their lands. To the marshal, Huter and his followers earnestly appealed, declaring it impossible to withdraw so rapidly without great loss and danger to those who were ill. They argued that it was against all justice to drive them out without sufficient reason, especially when no complaint had ever been made against them by the authorities. They offered to pay any tribute or taxes that he or the Prince might claim, if only they could be allowed to keep their work and their religion. This complaint was sent to the King. The only answer vouchsafed was: "Drive them out." So the marshal thought that he had no alternative, and his people came with drums and a little banner to the Brothers' settlement commanding them to quit. Huter led the way, followed by his assistant ministers, and then all the people with their children came out, two and two, following their shepherd like a flock of sheep going into the field. No resting place was allowed them in the marshal's lands, and with many weary efforts, they reached an open heath, where they encamped with a crowd of persons who needed looking after—widows and orphans, infirm and old people, and young children. It was amid this misery Huter wrote a well-known letter, the last cry of anguish of these cruelly persecuted people. Very truly could he describe the evicted families as persons who desired to do no man wrong, not even their most cruel enemy, as persons who would rather be robbed of hundreds of guilders than defraud anyone of a penny, who would rather be killed themselves than strike anyone a blow; yet he did not fail to assert, as a fundamental human right, the doctrine that the earth belongs to all, since it is the property of the Universal Father: "We know it is not allowable to forbid the earth to us, for the earth is the Heavenly Father's."

Ferdinand's answer was an order for the arrest of the courageous leader, and the brethren, notwithstanding the greatness of the sacrifice, urged Huter to leave them at once. After this, the wanderers, unwilling to separate, journeyed on, not knowing whither to go. All provision being at last refused them, even water, they were compelled to divide themselves into little groups, each led by some great-hearted Brother. The marshal von Lipa mercifully left the sick and aged, whom they could not venture to remove, in undisturbed possession of their former farm; but "the Holy Community" was destroyed. From a letter written to his wandering flock, it would seem that Huter only avoided capture by flying from one dangerous position to another. The joy of the Tyrolese Baptists at seeing him again was great; they worked and rejoiced as those who knew the time was short.

6

In the beginning of April, 1535, the warning went out: "Anabaptists from Moravia are roaming through the Tyrol." The frontiers were to be watched, and the districts where they were likely to enter. The same watch was to be kept on the Bavarian and Saxon frontiers, so that if the fugitive Baptists escaped one set of police, they fell into the hands of another. Notwithstanding the prodigious care taken to exclude these miserable outlaws, great numbers faun their way back into the Tyrol, and, to use the official expression, "spread and smuggled themselves over King Ferdinand's lands." As to Huter, he constantly held meetings in cellars or woods, and elsewhere, preaching with all the earnestness of a dying man to dying men.

The last three letters Huter wrote to the community in Moravia give a graphic idea of his terrible position, and the growing feeling of resentment which the absolute injustice of their treatment was impressing on the Anabaptist mind. "We have," he writes, "affliction and grief because the utmost iniquity and injustice have now got the upper hand. Nevertheless, the children of the Lord grow and increase in divine justice and truth, as a beautiful garden after a rain in May." "I would have you know," he says further on, "that we can no more be hidden. A great cry has gone against us, and the wicked priests—watchmen, and emissaries of the devil, cruel hell-hounds—cry out of the pulpit at us. The wicked Sodomitish sea tosses and rages. I much fear it will find no rest until the pious Jonah is cast forth and the cruel whale swallows him up." "Dearly loved brethren, we now expect daily, hourly, and at any moment, the police from the magistrates, and the executioners, soldiers, and every trouble." His last letter, forwarded to Moravia in November, 1535, by the brother Geronimus, concludes with the words: "Let us not be misled and frightened away from the divine Truth."

As on St. Andrew's Eve Huter went to Clausen to lodge for the night at a former mass priest's house, accompanied by his wife, then pregnant, he was in the stillness of the night suddenly arrested, and, with the priest's wife and a young girl, taken to prison. He was sent, escorted by an armed guard, to Innsbruck, his wife being detained at Clausen to be there examined. From her confession, it appears that she had not long been married to Huter and had followed him out of Moravia, escorted by the Brother Geronimus. She had come across the Tauern, probably by dangerous paths, and through scenes of savage grandeur, and, descending into the fertile valley of Taufers, had stayed a long time in the wood, fearing to enter the town. At the beginning of December, she was wandering with her husband, not knowing from hour to hour where God would lead them; penniless themselves, they lived by the aid of those also very necessitous.

It was severe winter weather when they led the captured leader, a gag in his mouth, to Innsbruck. A certain Dr. Gallen was called in to "instruct" him, but this proving waste of time, they put Huter to the torture, the result being that they were able to inform King Ferdinand that Huter denied the Church ordinances of Confession and the Holy Sacrament, but that it did not appear that he intended to plant Anabaptism in the Tyrol by force. They further intimate that they have discovered that he has been bishop and leader in Moravia, and they request that Tuchmacher (Hans Amon), Onoffrius, and Zaunried (Zaunring) may be arrested and imprisoned, so that they do not come privately and plant this sect among "the Common Man." They have also learned that in the Tyrol "the Common Man is so favorable to Huter as to have kept a great watch on his behalf, and that Huter solicits plate and trifles from him, which one may well suppose Huter has not shared with his Brothers and Sisters."

Soon after Christmas, the Government at Innsbruck was informed that it was the royal determination that Huter should be executed, whether he recanted or not; but whatever can be got out of him, which may cause the same fate to fall on others, is first to be extracted by torture. Racked in body and mind, the Anabaptist apostle lay for weeks in the Kräuterthurm; no impression, however, being made, it was determined to flog him; and soldiers expert in the art of flogging were ordered from Kufstein. But Huter was immovable and neither betrayed the faith nor his companions. On the 26th of January, at seven o'clock in the morning, he was again examined by torture. The Anabaptist histories relate that they placed him alternately in ice-cold water and then in a hot room;

that they beat him with rods, rubbing brandy into his inflamed wounds; but these statements of the histories Loserth speaks of as fabulous. "It is only certain," he concludes, "that Huter went through every form of the accustomed torture and remained firm until his end."

It was proposed that he should be executed in secret with the sword very early in the morning, but Ferdinand would in no way consent to this. Huter must die publicly and by fire. On Friday, 24th February, 1536, vast crowds assembled in Innsbruck, and the brave and faithful leader gave in his death as good an example as in his life.

With the death of Huter, the great time of the Tyrolese Anabaptism ends. Persistent persecution, with the destruction of the most energetic leaders, did the work, and Ferdinand I was successful.

Titles of Works Consulted

- Janssen, J.: *Geschichte des Deutschen Volkes seit dem Ausgang des Mittelalters.*

- Loserth, J.: *Anabaptismus in Tirol.*

- Loserth, J.: *Der Communismus der Mährischen Wiedertäufer.*

- Hast, J.: *Geschichte der Wiedertäufer.*

4

Anabaptism in Southern Germany and the Rhine Lands

1

When the persecution of the Baptists began in Switzerland, several of the leaders went into the south of Germany; among others Röubli, who early in 1525 arrived at Waldshut, a town in the Austrian dominions, and close to the Swiss frontier. The whole neighborhood was in insurrection, and Dr. Balthasar Hubmaier, preacher at Waldshut and an ardent reformer, had completely identified himself with the popular movement. Hubmaier had, for the greater part of his life, been an exemplary priest, and had as a preacher in the cathedral at Ratisbon denounced the iniquities of his time, and especially the practice of usury. Moreover, he always held that the Christian might use the sword, so that he was quite consistent when he took part in so just a cause as that of the German people against the many oppressions under which they suffered. After a disputation with Röubli, Hubmaier accepted believers' baptism and, with 110 others, was baptized in Passion week at a village near Waldshut. On Easter day he himself baptized some 300 persons.

When in November, 1525, Waldshut had to acknowledge the total defeat of the insurrection, Hubmaier sought refuge, as already related, in Switzerland, while Röubli went to Strassburg, whither, after making a visit to several places in Suabia, he again returned.

This city, so full of commercial life and energy, had always been an asylum for the persecuted. Here, as in Elsass generally, the members of such societies as the Brethren of the Free Spirit, the Friends of God, the Hidden Ones, etc., must have had scope for their activity. Such societies, or similar ones, were existing at, or shortly before, the time Anabaptism first made its appearance in these parts. From a document, dated Pentecost 1522, supposed to be written by Hartmuth von Cronberg, a friend of Sickingen, it appears that there was a society in Elsass calling itself the Divine Brotherhood, united on the ground of personal heartfelt faith and trust in Christ as Lord and Savior. Such faith, it asserted, can only be given by the grace of God, and those who possess it are thereby drawn together as brothers and sisters; and in no other way can anyone obtain a right to membership of the brotherhood. The taking of interest, receiving ground rents, or holding landed property, prevented admission into the brotherhood. Making provision for its poorer members was one of its chief considerations.

In Strassburg—which, according to Erasmus, ought to have been called Aurata, the city of gold, rather than Argentoratum, the city of silver—this gospel of the poor and unworldly had had voices even in high places. Geiler von Kaisersberg, preacher in the cathedral during the latter portion of the fifteenth century, was called "the Trumpet of Strassburg." He defended the rights of the people, denounced the way the rich worked the poor for their own advantage, and the unequal manner in which the burden of taxation was distributed. He was opposed to the chase, to all barbarous punishments, especially to torture; he showed great sympathy for those condemned to capital punishment, and for children abandoned by their parents; in fact, his love to the disinherited and outcast was such that he gave the whole of his salary as preacher to help them. The Reformers existed to make the spirit and tendencies of such men thoroughly triumphant in every department of the Church and State. This, at least, was what the People expected of them, and why they supported them.

With infinite pains and much patience, Martin Butzer succeeded in establishing a Zwinglian Church in Strassburg in union with the State and completely under the control of the authorities. This seemed to be politically advantageous for the city, which wished to keep in confederacy with the Swiss, but it was at the expense of suppressing or torturing the true conscience of Strassburg. Capito and Matthias Zell, his colleagues, were very different men and no doubt bewailed Butzer's habit of "taking more account of the circumstances of the time than of the truth."

Röubli was followed to Strassburg by these Baptist leaders: Jakob Gross of Waldshut, Pilgram Marbeck from the Tyrol, Michael Sattler, Ludwig Hetzer, and Hans Denck. Those who then led the Reformation in Strassburg gave them a friendly welcome. Zell was the most popular preacher in the city and a kind and just man. He declared from the pulpit that it was in harmony with the Baptist principle that the authorities have no right to use force in matters of faith. The influence of his wife was also entirely on the side of love and unity with the Baptists. Capito received Michael Sattler, Hetzer, and Cellarius into his own house and inclined to their views for a long time. Jakob Gross, the first to baptize in Strassburg on confession of faith, was with Michael Sattler appointed to the oversight of the Baptist community. Sattler sent the following creed to Capito and Butzer in the spring of 1527, and it may, no doubt, be accepted as the doctrine he taught his Brothers and Sisters in Strassburg:

1. Christ is come to save all who believe in Him;

2. Whosoever believes and is baptized is saved, whosoever believes not is condemned;

3. Faith in Christ Jesus reconciles us to the Father and makes a way to Him;

4. Baptism unites all believers unto the body of Christ;

5. Christ is the head of His body, that is, of believers, or the community;

6. What the head thinks, that also the members ought to think;

7. The foreseen, the called, the believing ought to be formed on the model of Christ;

8. Christ is in contempt in the world, so also are His own. He has no kingdom in this world, the worldly are against His kingdom;

9. The believing are chosen out of this world, therefore the world hates them;

10. The devil is prince over all the world, through him the children of darkness reign;

11. Christ is a spiritual prince; through Him live all who walk in the life;

12. The devil seeks to destroy, Christ to save;

13. The flesh strives against the spirit, and the spirit against the flesh;

14. The spiritual are of Christ, the fleshly for death and the wrath of God;

15. Christians are wholly passive and trust in the Heavenly Father in all outward and secular matters;

16. The citizenship of the Christian is in heaven, not on earth;

17. Christians are the companions of God and citizens of heaven, and not of the world;

18. But they are the true Christians who carry out the doctrine of Christ by acts;

19. Flesh and blood, custom and usage, are earthly, and the world is also not able to understand the Kingdom of Christ;

20. To sum up, there is nothing in common between Christ and Belial.[1]

---

1. Zar Geschichte der Strassburgischen Wiedertäufer von T. W, Röhrich, pp. 31, 32.

Sattler's stay in Strassburg was short—some inward motion drove him to martyrdom. He was succeeded by Pilgram Marbeck, whose remarkable character has been hidden under the subsequent ruin of his cause. Both in the Tyrol and at Strassburg, his position shows that he was highly thought of as an engineer. Here in Strassburg, he managed both the aqueduct and the rafts on the Rhine. Even Butzer testifies to the pious, irreproachable lives of Marbeck and his wife but adds, "This is an old bait of Satan, with which he has angled in all the churches."

But the teacher most feared in Strassburg was Hans Denck, whom Butzer styled "the Pope of the Anabaptists." Denck was, to use Vadian's description of him, a "remarkable young man," for despite his gentle, unassuming character, he was forced to fly from city to city, and his life soon came to an end. His strength lay in his mental grasp of the difficulties of Christian theology and the original solution he offered.

Lutherans and Zwinglians were at daggers drawn on sacramental questions, but on the most important points in theology, their difference was not great. But the Baptist, especially as represented by Denck, distinctly opposed Lutheran teaching on such points as justification, freewill, the relation of the law to the gospel, and holy scripture. The fundamental difference between Denck and Luther lay in the view each took of human nature; Denck affirmed that the human conscience contained a spark of the divine nature, so that God Himself might be said to be present in every man. To the urgings of this Inner Word, Denck affirmed a man could be obedient, and that such an act of obedience was an act of faith. For to Denck, this Inner Voice prompting to righteousness was no other than the Word of God, which in Christ became man, and which will to all eternity, as the spirit of love, work in man. Thus, to him, Christ had always lived in man, and ever will live in man, not merely figuratively, but in reality. Thus Denck could reconcile the statements of both the apostles—Paul and James—on justification, for the faith which Denck contended for was an act of obedience, essentially, therefore, a good work. His doctrine on this and every other point traversed the whole Lutheran ground, and either entirely opposed or gave a different explanation to such points as human depravity, election, free will, the future destiny of non-Christians and unbelievers, etc. Denck's view brought many non-Christians into the category of believers and placed many nominal Christians among the unbelievers. Denck, in fact, sought to get rid of unreality, the great curse of every form of Christianity.

His view with regard to the law was that Jesus Christ did not do away with it, but gave a deeper and wider meaning to it. Holy scripture, as containing the written Word of God, he regarded as the standard of faith, but the ground of faith he considered to be in the truths taught by experience. Faith thus arising found in holy scripture an educative and formative influence of the highest value. But holy scripture was not to be understood except by the help of the Holy Spirit and faithful obedience to the commands of Christ.

From this very brief summary, an idea may be formed of the advanced nature of the thought that pervaded South German Anabaptism at this period. From the testimony of contemporaries, it appears that there was then no other influence affecting the movement to be compared with that of Denck. As already said, Cellarius, the early adherent of the Zwickau prophets, was at Strassburg, in close intimacy with Capito, who greatly esteemed him. In a conference between Capito, Cellarius, and Derrek, Cellarius declared himself of Denck's views, and Capito was evidently inclined to do the same.

Butzer must have feared Denck's growing influence, for he proceeded to crush him according to the Zwinglian fashion. He arranged a public disputation, which took place on December 22, 1526. On the 23rd, Denck was ordered to at once quit Strassburg. To some, it may have appeared that this blow would drive the Baptists into insurrection, but Butzer, at least, knew the contrary, for he questioned Jakob Gross, who was imprisoned some time in 1526, and learnt that the latter would obey the authorities, except when called upon to act against the command of God and slay anyone.

Butzer, emboldened by the gentleness both of Jakob Gross and Capito, proceeded to represent to the authorities that the Baptists' doctrine consisted of three points: (1) To have no Government; (2) To do honor to no one; (3) To share their property with one another.

He also sent Zwingli a similarly distorted account of Denck's teaching: (1) Men can, by their own efforts, obtain justification before God;

(2) Sin is merely imaginary — that is, nothing at all; (3) Christ is simply an example in living a good life: He instills into us a determination to do right; (4) It is in the power of everyone to do right; (5) Men have free will.

Finally, in July 1527, no doubt under Butzer's influence, the Zwinglian clergy in Strassburg published a book against Denck's doctrine, entitled *The Warning of the Preachers of the Gospel at Strassburg.* Its text was a treatise on "Scripture, Infant Baptism, and Redemption by Christ," written by a disciple of Denck, Jacob Kautz of Worms.

Notwithstanding all this, and notwithstanding mandate after mandate from the authorities, the number of the Baptists in Strassburg continued during 1527 to increase. While the churches of the civic faith were deserted, the Baptists won numerous adherents among the young people of all classes. This condition alarmed the friends of Zwinglianism outside Strassburg as well as within. And all the more that the same falling away to the Baptists was seen in other cities.

2

Worms, where Jacob Kautz had been the Lutheran preacher before joining the Baptists, now became the asylum of the party. It was here on April 13th, 1527, that Denck and Hetzer published their translation of the prophetical books of Scripture, a translation which, according to Keller, formed the basis of both the Lutheran and Swiss translations.[2] It was so sought after and read that within thirteen years fifteen different issues appeared at Strassburg, Augsburg, Hagenau, etc., each issue going through a series of editions.

In Ulm, Ratisbon, and Nürnberg, the propaganda went on, and by the end of 1527, a network of communities existed in the cities of Upper Germany, the movement being greatly assisted by the writings of Hubmaier, Sattler, Denck, and Langenmantel. "The Baptist current," says Sebastian Franck, "swept swiftly throughout the whole land, many thousands were baptized, and many hearts drawn to them. For they

---

2. Keller: Ein Apostel der Wiedertäufer, p. 211.

taught nothing but love, faith, and crucifixion of the flesh, manifesting patience and humility under many sufferings, breaking bread with one another in sign of unity and love, helping one another with true helpfulness, lending, borrowing, giving, learning to have all things common, and calling each other 'brother.'"

It was not in the nature of things that the elevated religious thought of Denck should long prevail. The ever-growing intensity of the persecution destroyed the possibility of that calm reasonableness of temper which is its congenial atmosphere, and the only one in which it can bear perfect fruit.

Denck's fragile frame succumbed after two or three years' testimony, during which he was treated as if he were another Cain, and forced to fly—"a fugitive and a vagabond"—from place to place. Thus it came to pass that the Anabaptist mind fell back on longer received and more accredited forms of faith. And yet it is clear that Denck's theology was more distinctively Anabaptist than the creed just cited, and a great deal more so than that set forth at a later period in Münster by Rothmann and the Wassenberg preachers. The proof lying in this, that while those creeds say nothing of immediate revelation and the Inner Word, there was no doctrine more universally accepted and acted upon by all kinds of Anabaptists.[3]

How the life and progress to which Sebastian Franck refers maddened their enemies, begins to appear in the intense hatred and cruelty with which the Baptists now were pursued. Michael Sattler, one of the Baptist bishops at Strassburg, had not long left that city before he was arrested. From the Tower of Bintzdorp he wrote an epistle to the Church of God at Horb. Its burden is, "Flee the shadow of this world"—the reward being martyrdom in this world and the crown and palm of victory in the next. At the moment of writing Sattler was in expectation of soon realizing both. The town clerk at Ensisheim, where he appeared before his judges, was exceptionally brutal, continually saying, "Thou

---

3. For a fuller account of Denck's life and teaching see The Contemporary Review, December 1892: Hans Denck, the Anabaptist.

desperate wretch and arch-heretic;" while the martyr, with severe simplicity, addressing his judges, always said, "Ye servants of God." Upon this admirable Christian, one of the most faithful to be found in history the following sentence was passed: "That Michael Sattler be delivered over to the executioner, who shall bring him to the place of execution and cut out his tongue; he shall then throw him upon a cart, and twice tear his flesh with hot pincers; he shall then be brought to the city gate, and have his flesh five times torn in the same manner." And this sentence was carried out at Rothenberg, on the Neckar, May 25th, 1527, the martyr ending his testimony in the flames. Among those who suffered with Sattler, two at least were from Switzerland. A few days later they drowned his wife. These cruelties are inexplicable, until we recognize that the Baptists had the temerity to act as if the existing Christendom was not a Christian society after all, but still a province in the power and under the rule of "the Prince of this World."

The central point of the movement in Southern Germany was Augsburg. This imperial city acted as a link between Northern Germany and the Levant due to its association with Venice and Trieste. Its bankers and merchants had branches in the Adriatic, where they sent their young men to study the arts of commerce. An idea of the opulent lifestyle enjoyed by Augsburg citizens can be gleaned from their extensive time spent in baths. The affluent youth of German cities would frequently bathe three times a day. According to entries in the diary of an Augsburg citizen, it is evident that in the span of three weeks, he spent 157 hours in the baths, which amounts to approximately seven to eight hours per day. Meals and drinks were consumed during bathing sessions. Sensuality and debauchery were particularly fashionable during this period, and it can be assumed that the debauched living style described by Kriegk in his *Deutsches Bürgertum* was rampant in Augsburg, as well as in other cities. After three or four years of experience, Urbanus Rhegius declared that he must leave Augsburg. Its pride, vain glory, and worldliness were unbearable. Huberinus, another Lutheran clergyman, stated in 1531 that decency and honor are no longer observed in Augsburg. All kinds of unchasteness and licentiousness seem to have gained the upper hand. "If things go on like this," said another preacher from the pulpit in 1526, "it would be better to fight one another to the death; I have got my little knife with me."

When Denck arrived in Augsburg in the summer or autumn of 1526, a Baptist community had already been formed there by Jakob Gross of Waldshut and Caspar Ferber from the Innthal. It was the direct offspring of the communities in Switzerland and the Tyrol. The same fact was more or less the case in many places, and helps us to understand how the indignation aroused by the relation of the martyrdoms in the Tyrol and in Switzerland would spread over the German-speaking lands. For the people must have felt that they were blows struck at their own faith.

Denck himself had not yet been baptized as a full believer, but in Augsburg, he felt moved to do what he could to stop the moral fall of the city, and nothing appeared so likely to effect that object as "a fellowship of the saints."

Hubmaier, after leaving Zürich and Constance, arrived at Augsburg, where he was the means of deciding Denck to join the brotherhood. Denck, baptized, at once became an active member of the community. In the spring of 1527, he baptized Hans Hut, who had formerly taken part in the Peasant War. The form of baptism carried out in Augsburg was not, as at Münster and elsewhere, by sprinkling, or as among the Mennonites, by affusion, but by immersion, the men being naked, the women clad in a gown.[4]

This fact, which seems well authenticated, would suggest that the mode was the same throughout South Germany, Switzerland, and the Tyrol since the Augsburg community was founded by the Waldshuter Jakob Gross and the Tyrolese Ferber. Moreover, Augsburg appears to have been the most important Baptist center in South Germany. By the end of 1527, the number of the community there had reached 1,100.

It is evident that immediately after the bloody close of the Peasant War, a most indefatigable missionary work took place in all parts of

---

4. Keller: Ein Apostel der Wiedertäufer, p. 112. In a note, Dr. Keller states that this fact rests on the tradition of an eyewitness who is to be trusted, the Augsburg Benedictine Sender.

Germany, so that the desire for justice, the motive power of the insurrection, was carried into lands that hitherto had not felt it in this ardent form. How numerous the apostles must have been we gather from the evidences of their work. How did they escape detection and arrest? Perhaps they made use of the great rivers and their many affluents. On those silent highways, there were no roving *landsknechte*, no soldiers, no police, no spies. Their little boats shot down with the stream, and it was difficult to discover or pursue them. Thus, at this time, we hear not only of this great community at Augsburg but of others at Passau, Salzburg, and Munich. Salzburg, where the Baptists were called garden-brethren, from their custom of meeting in a garden and other solitary places at night, was the scene of a series of martyrdoms during 1527 and 1528. A priest and three other persons were put in a meeting house, which was then set on fire, and later, we read of a grand holocaust in which eighteen persons were burnt together—for nothing, says the narrative, but that they "confessed Christ to be Lord alone, and would not honor the image, nor worship the beast." At Munich in February 1527, George Wagner was put to death. He was visited in prison by persons in high position who urged him to recant. When in the flames, he often repeated the name of Jesus, it having been agreed that he should give this sign of unshaken faith.

The pastors at Augsburg were two former monks—Salminger from Munich and Dachsen from Ingolstadt. They composed hymns, as also did Hans Hut, Hetzer, and Langenmantel. In the state archives at Augsburg is a little half-torn hymn book which, besides other things, contains examples of the kind of hymns which these men wrote.

In the autumn of 1527, an Anabaptist Synod or Conference was held at Augsburg. Sixty deputies were present, with Denck presiding. Some are said to have wished to revert to Müntzer's line of action, but if so, they were not supported by the assembly. It was decided that Christians should not obtain power by unlawful means. Apostles were sent out in various directions. Derek's little book on "True Love" is said to have been intended as a sort of confession of faith to be disseminated among the brothers far and near. This Assembly has been named the Martyr Synod because many of its members died for the cause. Schiemer, Schlaffer,

Schneider, Thomas (Waldhauser), Hetzer, Hans Hut, Prader, and Beck were all present, and each has a place in Van Braght's martyrology.[5]

3

The German Baptists during this period ardently desired to reproduce the time when the apostles, wandering from town to town, formed the first Christian communities, uniting all in brotherly love as members of one body. Taking into account the differences of country and time, they sent forth men of the same order. These men went to the downtrodden and needy, for it was to such that the Lord had sent them. "Peace be to this house," they said as they entered the laborer's hut, and then proceeded to speak of the evils of this world and the need for deeds of love, reading and explaining the Scriptures. Mutual love and joy were the reward. To the apostles, these poor homes were illuminated by the presence of God, while to their humble hosts, there was something poignant in the words of men upon whose heads the halo of a martyr's crown seemed to hover. Hans Hut enters Franz Stiegel's house at Weier, in Franconia, reads God's word, and speaks of baptism. Stiegel and eight others are baptized, and the same night Hans Hut goes on his way, never having seen before or seeing since those he baptized.

The memory of the words thus spoken often left souls restless as Noah's dove, striving in the blinding mist to find its way to the ark of refuge. Cornelius relates an incident which recalls the flight of Christian from the City of Destruction. In the dead of the night the peasant Hans Rer, at Alten-Erlangen, rose up from his bed and felt for his clothes and traveling things. "Where art thou going?" asked his wife. "I know not," he answered, "God knows." "What have I done to grieve thee," she said; "remain here and help me to bring up the little children." "Dear wife,"

---

5. Preface to a modern edition of Hans Denck's little tract, "Von der wahren Liebe," Mennonitische Verlagshandlung, Elkhart, Indiana.

he replied, "leave me unburdened by earthly things. God bless thee; I will from henceforth know and do the will of God."[6]

Such people gathered into a community, which they believed was the body of Christ. This idea was not peculiar to them; but while other religious communities held it theoretically, these poor people sought to make it a reality. Hence their desire to separate as much as possible from the world; for the more they mingled with the world, the more unreal their ideal became. Certain fashions of the world always tended to its destruction: great disparity in wealth and social rank, that kind of patriotism which made the slaughter of men in other lands in the interest of one's own a prime duty, that kind of loyalty which required men to swear obedience to other authorities than Christ. But they found no place or society free from these things, therefore they not only avoided the ordinary haunts of worldly people, but even guild halls and civic meetings. To them all things were either good or bad; all men belonged either to the kingdom of darkness or to the kingdom of light, to Christ or to Belial. For every member of the one only Divine society they cultivated love, regarding them as children of their Father and co-proprietors in all they possessed. They dressed with similar plainness, they called each other brother and sister, and kissed when they met.

The central point of their worship, and the keystone of their social order, was the Lord's Supper. They celebrated it first of all as a memorial of Christ's death; but also as a renewal of the covenant with God, and in order to strengthen love among themselves. Participating in it was regarded as a solemn engagement not to separate in any calamity; not to vex one another; to have all things spiritual and temporal in common; to pray for enemies and to do them good; and so to maintain the covenant with God as long as life lasted. If danger or persecution threatened,

---

6. "So I saw in my dream that the man began to run. Now he had not gone far from his own door, when his wife and children perceiving it, began to cry after him to return; but the man put his fingers in his ears, and ran on, crying Life! Life! Eternal Life!" (The Pilgrim's Progress).

communion in the Lord's Supper was felt to be a consecration and an inspiration. Only in willingness to give oneself up to the Lord under the cross could anyone rightly partake of the Lord's Supper. Bread and wine were, above all, signs of the collective sufferings and unity, and often led the preacher to dwell on the thought that, as bread through water and the heat of the oven was made out of many corns, and as out of many berries wine through the press, so must the members of the Community be formed into one life through suffering.

The Brothers ascribed to the State no Christian character, but regarded it as belonging with the whole unbelieving world to the kingdom of darkness. For true Christians, magistrates were unnecessary, but if they were persecuted by them, they must pray for them and endure it. The time will come when it will be quite otherwise. The two kingdoms were already in opposition, there could be no doubt which would conquer.

Such doctrines brought upon the Anabaptists the hostility of the authorities in every State in Germany, and ultimately wherever they were found throughout Europe. The Catholic rulers in Germany were the first to treat Anabaptism as a capital crime, and the blood of the Baptists flowed like water in the Catholic States. But the Protestant rulers, having accepted the idea that force might be used in the cause of the Gospel, soon joined in the exterminatory work.

If any of the local authorities had had any doubt as to their legal right to proceed to the most extreme form of persecution, it was removed by the Imperial mandate of January 4, 1528. In Augsburg, where in 1527 they had begun by flogging Baptists out of the city, and cutting out the tongue of one of them, they now beheaded another—Liepolt Schneider. How courageously these Baptists met their fate may be seen in the exhortation Hansken von Stotzingen made to the people as he was led to execution at Saberen (Saverne), in Elsass, "Be courageous and undaunted, thou little worm Jacob! Although Pharaoh seeks thy life, it is nevertheless a light affliction. The Red Sea will open. Does Pharaoh pursue thee? He shall there come to his end."

At the second Diet of Speyer, March 1529, a resolution was adopted commanding the magistrates that every Anabaptist, male or female, of ripe years and understanding, should be put to death by fire, sword, or otherwise, and be in no other way judged or dealt with, under pain of heavy and severe judgment.

The results of these edicts are to be seen in the number of executions which now took place. "In a few years," says Sebastian Franck, speaking of this time, "some 2,000 or more Baptists are estimated to have been put to death. In some places, the slaughter amounted to wholesale massacre. Up to the year 1531, there were killed in Ensisheim 600 Baptists; in Linz, 73; in the Palatinate, 350, many of whom were put to death at Alzey. The numerous executions in Suabia did not satisfy the Suabian League, for they sent out armed troopers to scour the country," and the leaders were given authority to hunt the fanatics like wild beasts, and at once, *without law or trial*, to put them to death.

In Bavaria, where the Baptists were very numerous, the Duke ordered that those who recanted should be beheaded, and those who did not should be burned. The Austrian Government beheaded those taken on the high road, and they hung on their own doorposts those taken in the villages. Among seven who died together at Gmünd in 1529 was a lad of fourteen years of age, a servant. He lay a whole year in prison with unshaken faith. As he was waiting his turn to be beheaded, a count rode into the ring and said to him: "My dear child, if you will give up these errors, I will maintain you and have you always with me." The boy martyr replied: "Were I to love my life and forsake my God, in order to escape this cross, it would serve me little. Your treasures can profit neither of us; I look for better in heaven." Amid such exciting scenes, the legendary soon formed itself in the poetic soul of the people. When Leonhard Kayser was being taken to execution at Schärding, in Bavaria, he bent over one side of the cart and plucked a flower, saying to the judge: "If you can burn me and this flower, then have you righteously condemned me; but otherwise, if you can neither burn me, nor this flower in my hand, then reflect on what you have done and repent." And it is related that, do what they would, his body could not be consumed, but when the ashes were brushed away, the skin was smooth and clear, and the flower found unfaded in his hand and not in the least burned.

4

When Anabaptism was thus dying down in Southern Germany, a man appeared in Strassburg who infused into it a new character, and gave it an extraordinary impetus in the northwest of the Empire. Melchior Hoffmann is first heard of as a furrier in Waldshut, whence, under the influence of the religious movement of the time, he went forth to preach at Zürich. "The good-for-nothing fellow who prepares skins," wrote Zwingli to Valiant, in 1523, "has begun to play the evangelist in this place and questions me." Hoffmann went about from one part of Europe to the other preaching without fee or reward, supporting himself by his handicraft. His preaching was welcomed by the people, although he would seem to have been far more interested in the things that were coming upon the earth than in any efforts to improve existing social conditions. But the firm conviction he had that the world lay captive in bondage to Satan, and that he was called to awaken men to the miseries this had brought upon them, and would bring upon them, led to much the same result. And thus, though he upheld obedience to the authorities, allowed the using of weapons, and the taking of oaths on exceptional occasions,[7] he did not escape becoming a popular hero.

In company with Knipperdolling, a merchant from Münster, Hoffmann went in a Dutch vessel to Sweden, whence he was driven away by the clergy. A thoroughly disinterested man, he had no doubt of his calling to the prophetical office. Neither opposition nor suffering dismayed him. In times when all things seemed rocking, a man so eloquent, so full of faith, so confident that he could explain from the Scriptures the meaning of the crisis, could not fail to attract a great following. Driven from Lübeck, Hoffmann went to Holstein, where King Frederick of Denmark not only gave him protection but a living and freedom to preach throughout Holstein. A Lutheran at this time, Hoffmann went to Wittenberg, and obtained Luther's approval and support. But his

---

7. Cornelius: Geschichte des Münsterischen Aufruhrs. Vol. II, p. 94.

Bible studies led him eventually to give up the Lutheran idea of the Lord's Supper, and, as a consequence, he was driven from Denmark, just as he had been from other places. Carlstadt came to his aid and gave him an asylum. He arrived at Strassburg, where he met Schwenkfeld, and to conversation with him, or to misconception of his ideas on the humanity of Christ, Hoffmann's strange doctrine on the Incarnation has been attributed.

Butzer welcomed him at first as a sufferer for Zwinglianism, but soon ceased to be his friend, and possibly in the message Hoffmann received from the Council, to "give up preaching and mind his own business," Butzer's influence may be seen. But Hoffmann soared far above such impertinences. He did not deny the office of the regularly ordained ministry; but between it and the ministry he exercised there was, he said, just the difference that lies between the nominal and the real. The authorized preachers were no doubt the appointed watchmen in Jerusalem; but if the Bride, seeking the Bridegroom, were to ask them if they had seen her Beloved, they must reply: "We have not seen Him, nor do we even know Him."

Hoffmann's views as to the things coming on the earth, taking the forms of a time when men were unusually alive to social as well as theological questions, fell like seeds of fire into thousands of human hearts. Whether he would or no, his expositions of prophecy could not fail to have a social and political meaning. Nor could a man of his sympathetic nature and his struggling life, however much he may have lived in the oratory and in the study, have failed himself to be affected by the social-democratic sentiment which in German lands then dominated the common human heart.

About the year 1539 Hoffmann definitely joined the Baptist community in Strassburg, and in a few months is seen actively engaged as an apostle and a baptizer. His adhesion meant no surrender of his own peculiar views; on the contrary, the Baptists more and more surrendered their views to his, so that the direction of the whole movement began to change remarkably. While agreeing with the Brothers and Sisters as to believers' baptism and the necessity of maintaining a pure society apart from that of the world, and while opposing as they did the Lutheran teaching on justification, free will, and election, Hoffmann practically denied the position of the early Baptists, that the members of Christ's Kingdom could not serve or defend the kingdoms of this world, since he permitted the use of the sword and oath-taking. It is noteworthy that this attitude of Hoffmann with regard to weapon-bearing was that of Hubmaier, who was probably his early teacher. Hubmaier, Cornelius says, at the time of the peasant rising stood at the gate of the city watchhouse in Waldshut, a great broadsword in his hand, and wrote the famous twelve articles.[8] This recognition that the Kingdom of Heaven and the kingdoms of this world were so far one that a servant of the former could serve in the latter, even to the extent of taking an oath and of being ready at their bidding to draw the sword, was entirely to shift the ground on which Anabaptism stood; it was, in fact, to take the ground of its opponents, that the kingdoms of this world are in a subordinate sense the Kingdom of God, and that their rulers are His viceregents on earth. But the vast bulk of the Anabaptists believed just the opposite, and not only Hoffmann's prophetical teaching, but events also, daily strengthened them in their belief. If then they gave up their objection to the methods of this world's kingdoms—fighting and covenanting by oath-taking—how could it end otherwise than in their using these methods in defense of the Kingdom of Heaven and against the kingdoms of this world? And this was what did happen.

Another very serious deviation Hoffmann introduced was the strange notion that Christ did not take His flesh from Mary, but that the Word itself without any human intervention became flesh. "The Saviour," he said, "passed through the Virgin Mary as sunshine through a pane of glass." But it was his doctrine of the Last Things which most rapidly affected the Baptist movement and rendered it more and more visionary. Hoffmann taught that the whole course of the world unto the last days was revealed in Holy Scripture, and that to understand it all that was needed was diligent investigation and prayer—a very different doctrine from that of Hans Denck.

---

8. Cornelius: Geschichte des Münsterischen Aufruhrs. Vol. II, p. 104.

According to Hoffmann, the last seven years of the world had arrived, and the last preaching office was being carried on. It was the period of the Two Witnesses, and when their testimony was ended, a period of peace and abundance would come. Until then, luxury and pleasure would dominate the earth, doctrine be again darkened by glosses, a third part of the teachers drawn down earthward, and the devil again seduce the world so that the Elect would hardly stand. There would be a council of the apostolical teachers; the Cross and suffering, the sign of the Son of Man, would fall on the saints; the slaughter among the Elect would be great, and no one will dream that Christ is at hand. And so the spiritual temple built in a time of anxiety, as Zerubbabel's temple, will be destroyed. Then will the Son of Man appear in clouds from heaven.

Hoffmann's doctrines were decidedly opposed by a section of the Baptist community at Strassburg, who held fast to the teaching of Kautz and Röubli and separated from the Melchiorites, as Hoffmann's followers were called. It was not, however, as successful as the opposition had been at Augsburg and Nikolsburg to the prophetical expositions of Hans Hut. After the famous victories resulting from Hoffmann's new campaign in East Friesland and the Netherlands,[9] the Melchiorites gained ascendancy in Strassburg. The enthusiasm increased. "The time," he said, "had again returned when the young men and maidens should prophesy, and the old men see visions and dream dreams." Prophets and prophetesses arose in the Strassburg community, and Hoffmann expounded their revelations. He was regarded as Elias, and Strassburg as the New Jerusalem, into which the hundred and forty-four thousand were to be gathered.

This visionary tendency was calamitous for the whole brother-and-sisterhood in South Germany, and Strassburg became the last spot where they had any sure foothold. On Hoffmann's return from his fourth missionary tour, he was thrown into prison. Somewhat mildly treated at first, his imprisonment became very severe due to an attempt to escape. After some years, his sufferings ended, and his ardent soul passed

---

9. See below, pp. 82ff (chapter 5, section 2).

from the power of his torturers. The exact date is unknown, and perhaps he had been dead for some time before the fact was discovered by the jailers.

Titles of Works Consulted

- Rohrich, T. W.: *Zur Geschichte der Strassburger Wiedertäufer.*

- Cornelius, C. A.: *Geschichte des Münsterischen Aufruhrs.*

- Janssen, J.: *Geschichte des Deutschen Volkes.*

- Stähelin, A.: *Die Sozialen der Reformationszeit.*

- Keller, L.: *Ein Apostel der Wiedertäufer.*

- Brons, A.: *Ursprung, Entwicklung und Schicksale der Taufgesinnten oder Mennoniten.*

- Herrmann, G.: *Essai sur la vie et les écrits de Melchior Hofmann.*

- Van Braght: *Het Bloedig Tooneel, etc.*

- *Underhill's Martyrology of the Churches of Christ commonly called Baptists.*

5

Anabaptism in the Netherlands

1

The Netherlanders were a people well prepared for Anabaptism. For not only had they been peculiarly open to all the influences which kept alive in medieval Christendom the desire for a better representation of the Kingdom of God, but they had had the advantage of being educated by the universally honored society, "The Brothers of the Common Life." Within a year after the establishment of the Brothers at Deventer (about 1383) they had settlements in some twenty of the principal towns of the Netherlands, and their schools were erelong to be found in every part of the land. At Zwolle they had 800 scholars, at Alkmaar 900, at Hertogenbosch, 1,200; at Deventer, towards the end of the fifteenth century, the number reached 2,200. The education they gave was emphatically Christian, for it was an axiom with the founder of the society "that the root of study and the mirror of life must, in the first place, be the Gospel of Christ."

They wrote against the Church rule, which forbade Bible-reading, contending for the Scriptures in the vulgar tongue. They circulated the New Testament, supported themselves by making copies of the Bible, and read the Gospels aloud in the vulgar tongue to assemblies of adults, explaining what was read.

Thus, while under influences somewhat similar to those described in previous chapters as demoralizing the whole German empire, and as specially depressing the poor, the Netherlanders had been educated to value the Scriptures, and for the first time had come to possess them in their own tongue. The first translation of the Bible appeared in 1477 at Delft; but the spreading of Luther's books, and the universal desire throughout the Empire for a reform in Church and State led, between 1523 and 1531, to the production of more than twenty-five translations in the Netherlands of the Bible. The Bible was just the Book the people wanted, for it gave a standard for the reform they were seeking: a reform at once social, political, and religious.

The vast majority of those who desired reform stayed in the church of Rome until a moment came when conscience compelled them openly to declare by word or deed that they separated themselves from what they had come to consider no church at all. But most people were slow to take this final step; it would even seem that some received the new doctrine not only without ceasing outwardly to be members of their old communion, but even without ceasing to officiate as priests and to preach in the parish churches.

Sympathy with the idea of reformation affected all sorts and conditions of people, except the highest ruling class. The magistrates at Amsterdam and Delft were distinctly favorable to the popular movement. The edicts of the Court at Brussels were evaded by the civic authorities at Amsterdam: either they did not put the edicts in force, or they privately warned those to be arrested; or when the prisoners were actually before them, they made the punishment as slight as possible.

To prevent this widespread movement from developing into irresistible proportions, the Emperor issued ordinance after ordinance of a more and more penal character. The whole country was put under a delegation of lawyers empowered to arrest suspected persons, imprison them, bring them to justice, and see that the sentences were executed. In the course of the year 1522, the imperial edict began to be put in operation in Holland, and in 1523, the campaign was opened against the New Testament and all Reformation literature. In the spring of 1523, an edict appeared ordering all such books to be given up within eight days under heavy penalties. Another soon followed to stop their being printed in the Netherlands, and in the autumn of the same year, both ordinances were made more severe. Charles V was in dire earnest, and the Regent

Margaretha herself appeared at The Hague and heard accusations against heretics from all parts of the province.

However, the utmost the Emperor succeeded in doing was to break the opposition of the magistrates in Dutch cities and to drive a considerable number of leading Lutherans into exile. Until 1525, there were no cases of capital punishment, but the great insurrection in that year in Germany changed this. The first martyr for the reformed doctrine was Willem Dirks, a cooper, of Utrecht; the second was the Lutheran preacher, Jan Bakker, who on September 15, 1525, was burnt at The Hague. On the 17th, another prisoner from Woerden suffered: a widow, described as "Weynken Olaes' daughter." She went to her death as to a festival. That the nature of her faith was Anabaptist is seen in her reply to the monk in attendance who, holding up the crucifix, said, "Look once on your Lord who died for you." "That is not the Lord my God," she replied, "the Lord my God is in me, and I am in Him." The next who suffered, Jan Walen, and two companions were sentenced at Haarlem to a form of suffering which might well terrify the bravest of men. They were bound with chains to stakes and slowly roasted to death.

The early martyrdom or flight of the few eminent persons who held Lutheran ideas left the Netherlanders more free to develop their own native sentiments, and these tended to views on the sacraments more like those of Zwingli than of Luther. This tendency has been attributed to the teaching of the Brothers of the Common Life. In any case, the tendency took an independent course of its own, with other influences coming through the same source that equally affected the popular mind. The *Imitatio Christi* as the "Pilgrim's Progress," was the concentrated experience of generations. Thomas à Kempis had not only learned much from communion, both silent and spoken, with his spiritual brothers, but perhaps he had already absorbed the spirit of his future work in the home of his childhood. For certainly in "The Imitation," we have the essence of the deeper contemplations of medieval Holland, divinely mystical, as were those who meditated on these things and pondered them in their hearts. The imitation or following after Christ was always a central concept in the Baptist creed, especially in its earlier and purer forms. Hoffmann and Matthysz, no more than Sattler, Grebel, Denck,

Hubmaier, Huter, or Menno, would have given any but a secondary place to adult baptism. Its binding force lay in the very fact that it was following Christ, a direct imitation of His example. The fact that Christ Himself neither practiced nor commended infant baptism was an insurmountable objection to its continuation in their view.

2

In 1529 the Reform movement had so progressed that the charge of heresy was brought against all the cities in Holland, and the higher ruling powers grew more alarmed and more severe. The usual results followed. All who had reason to fear, and had the means to fly the country, did so. It was not, however, very easy, as every avenue of escape was closed, except in the direction of East Friesland.

Unlike most of the little sovereigns, the rulers of East Friesland—Count Edzard, and his adviser Ulrich von Dornum—were tolerant of all modes of religious thinking. The way from Holland, moreover, was a well-beaten line of traffic, making a journey in the direction of East Friesland natural and unsuspicious. Thus East Friesland soon became a haven of refuge for fugitives in trouble because of their interest in reform, such people flying there from all parts of the German empire.

In the year 1528 numbers came from the Upper Rhine and the Oberland, who were doubtless much more distinctly Baptist than those who, up to that date, had come out of the Netherlands. These fugitives preferred to meet in private houses rather than churches, and to be addressed by laymen rather than clergymen. Other signs of Baptist tendencies appear—difficulties about oaths and magistrates. It was even said that "hearing and believing must go before baptizing;" that in two years the Lord would come and fight with the princes of this world, that the wicked would be destroyed, and the Elect reign with the Lord.

Thus East Friesland was, in many ways, well prepared for the Baptist propaganda, and it seemed as if Anabaptism was about to become the leading influence when Count Edzard died. He was succeeded by his son Enno, whose policy was to bring about one uniform State Church, which, for political reasons, he wished to be Lutheran. However, as the people inclined to Zwinglianism, if not Anabaptism, it was difficult to do more than ruin the old Church, which was done in the iniquitous fashion of the English religious revolution. A commission was appointed to superintend the confiscation of the lands and other valuables collected by the former clergy; the churches and convents were ransacked, and the commissioners "making"—according to Beninga, the old East Friesland chronicler—"the best use of the time; each grabbed with covetous hands." Count Enno, of course, received the largest portion. He converted the Dominican monastery at Norden into a new residence and the Benedictine monastery at Ihlow into a hunting castle.

Into the midst of this den of thieves came Hoffmann, and the contrast between such a lofty poetic nature and that of the ducal reformer was manifest. The people flocked to him, the Count and the great men of East Friesland bent before him. Derided at Strassburg, he was all-powerful at Emden, baptizing 300 persons in the sacristy of the great church. How many elsewhere we are not told. His progress was evidently a triumphal march, and suggestive, even if legendary, is the story that his exhortations moved Count Enno to tears. In any case, no difficulties seem to have been put in the way of those he gathered into a community. Aportanus, one of the authorized preachers at Emden and formerly tutor to the children of Count Edzard, even thought the Baptist community there might be as useful an example as that of the Brothers of the Common Life at Zwolle. Concerning the ordering of this community, Hoffmann said, "God's community knows no head but Christ. No other can be endured, for it is a brother-and-sisterhood. The teachers have none who rule them spiritually but Christ. Teachers and ministers are not lords. The pastors have no authority except to preach God's word and punish sins. A bishop must be elected out of the community. Where a pastor has thus been taken, and the guidance committed to him and to his deacon, a community should provide properly for those who help to build the Lord's house. When teachers are thus found, there is no fear that the communities will suffer spiritual hunger. A true preacher would willingly see the whole community prophesy."

In the selection of a pastor to lead the Emden community, no doubt these principles were put into practice. Jan Volkertz, also known as

Trijpmaker due to his occupation in plush-making, did not occupy this position for long; for on January 19th, 1530, Count Enno decreed the expulsion of all Anabaptists. Volkertz went to Amsterdam, where he founded a Baptist community, which Hoffmann visited in 1530, undoubtedly participating in its Bible readings, baptisms, communions, marriages, and other communal activities. Hoffmann's teachings now spread not only in Amsterdam but throughout Holland, Zeeland, Friesland, and beyond, exerting influence on the entire Baptist party. This new form of Anabaptism became known to the Court of Holland, and those who embraced Hoffmann's ideas were distinguished as Melchiorites. The *schout*, the head of the police in Amsterdam, was ordered in 1532 to prosecute them. Volkertz voluntarily presented himself to the authorities, who then sent him to The Hague. Meanwhile, warned by the young wife of the *schout*, most of the others fled, resulting in only nine individuals being apprehended. By explicit order of the Emperor, they were beheaded at The Hague, and their heads were sent in a herring barrel to Amsterdam. There, they were placed on stakes in a circle, with the head of the pastor in the center above the others. This gruesome spectacle was arranged to be seen by ships returning home or departing. The *schout* refused to go near the location, while the burgomaster openly and fearlessly expressed his indignation. Under these circumstances, the fugitives dared to return, but Hoffmann sent them a message to remain quiet and abstain from baptizing for two years.

Hoffmann commenced his apostolate in the Netherlands by the publication of a book, written in Dutch, entitled "The Ordinances of God." The words of Christ to His disciples, "All power is given unto Me in heaven and on earth. Go ye therefore and teach all nations, baptizing them in the name of the Father, and of the Son, and of the Holy Ghost; teaching them to observe all things whatsoever I have commanded you; and lo, I am with you always, even unto the end of the world,"—apply, said Hoffmann, to the present time. "Christ, King in heaven and on earth, sends His friends and servants to teach all nations that He has sacrificed Himself for the whole world and taken away its sins. It is the work of a true apostle, not only to proclaim this Gospel of the Crucified, but also to bring to all people the joyful kiss from the mouth of the

Bridegroom, who has been made by His Father king over all creatures in heaven and earth, and to deliver the message that all those who serve Him and will acknowledge Him as Lord can come to Him freely and surely, and that He will keep them with Him eternally. And the messengers of the Lord are further commanded to unite to Christ through baptism all who have thus given Him their hearts. To the Bride (the holy community formed of those who have thus given themselves in baptism) the Bridegroom gives Himself in bread and wine, as an earthly bridegroom gives himself with a ring; and the Bride, receiving the bread and wine, through faith becomes with the Bridegroom one body and one flesh, one spirit and one mind."

But these high thoughts were obscured by Hoffmann's prediction that the end of all things was at hand. Strassburg, according to him, had been chosen as the New Jerusalem; there the magistrates would set up the kingdom of righteousness, while the hundred and forty and four thousand would maintain the power of the City, and the true Gospel and the true Baptism would spread over the earth. No man would be able to withstand the power, signs and wonders of the saints; and with them would appear, like two mighty torches, Enoch and Elias, who would consume the earth with the fire proceeding from their mouths. The year 1533 was the time in which, Hoffmann declared, the great fulfillment would begin.

Hoffmann's imprisonment at Strassburg, so far from effecting the object of the Council, was regarded by the Melchiorites as proof of the truth of their leader's mission. It had, they said, all been expected. Nor did the faith of the imprisoned prophet lessen. "O ye beloved saints of God and zealous members of Christ," he wrote from prison to his followers, "raise your heads, hearts, eyes, and ears, for the redemption is at hand. All the plagues are given over to the seventh angel of vengeance. When this angel has completed his work, when the firstborn of Egypt are smitten, when the kingdoms of Babylon and Sodom have come to an end, then will the joyful Alleluia be sung, the spiritual Samson and Jonah will come forth, and the spiritual Joseph and Solomon will again exercise lordship in the power of God over the whole earth."

3

The ghastly fate of Volkertz and his fellow Melchiorites was preceded and followed by other Anabaptist martyrdoms. The state of indignation which these things wrought in a people outwardly calm, but of intense inward feeling, took form, and men arose in Holland to give Melchioritism a powerful impulse and another direction, such as Hoffmann had given to Anabaptism. The year 1533 was almost at an end, the half-year during which it had been prophesied Hoffmann should be imprisoned had nearly elapsed, the two years' cessation from baptism had nearly run out, when a new prophet arose, who claimed to be the second witness of whom Hoffmann had spoken.[1] The underground fires had been gathering force, and they found their vent in a man who had spent his days in kneading the dough, watching for it to ferment and then casting it into the oven. Jan Matthysz, of Haarlem, was a man of the mold of Calvin or Knox, without their learning or knowledge of the world. His first appearance aroused some resistance, the community in Amsterdam being unwilling to recognize any rival to Melchior, their teacher and prophet. But the strong will and powerful character of the new prophet soon overcame all opposition.

The Dutch Baptists felt that a leader had risen up amongst them, and they yielded themselves to his guidance. Matthysz began by sending out apostles. Gerrit Boeckbinder and Jan Beukelsz, of Leiden, went to Münster; Dirk Kuyper and Bartholomeus Boeckbinder went to Leeuwarden, arriving there in the autumn of 1533. They sought out the Melchiorites and others inclined to them, and having ordained Obbe Philipsz and Hans Barbier, went on. In a short time Matthysz sent another apostle, Pieter Houtzager, to Leeuwarden, who eight days after baptized Dirk Philipsz. These apostles went forth announcing, among other things, that the promised time had come, that no more Christian blood would be poured out, but that in a short time God would overthrow the tyrants

---

1. See above, p. 76.

and bloodshedders with all the rest of the wicked. They traveled through many States and visited many cities, going to the gatherings of the faithful and offering them the kiss of peace. They baptized and ordained bishops and deacons, committing to the former the duty of ordaining others.

The new tide of enthusiasm rose higher than ever. Jakob van Kampen, who, assisted by Houtzager, worked among the poorer homes in Amsterdam, baptized in February, 1534, in one day a hundred persons. About two months later it was estimated that two-thirds of the population at Monnikendam were adherents of Jan Matthysz, and it is said to have been the same in the neighborhood of most of the great cities of Holland. Kennemerland, Amstelland, and Waterland were reported to be deeply infected; in Westzaandam the Baptists were reckoned at 200. It was the same with the chief places in West Friesland and Overyssel. In Deventer the burgomaster, Jacob van Winsum, was baptized. Deventer, the original home of the Brothers of the Common Life, was with its sister cities, Zwolle and Kampen, so thoroughly one with the movement that, with Amsterdam and Strassburg, it came to be looked upon as one of the cities God was about to give the saints. Hertogenbosch, another important center of the influence of the Brothers of the Common Life, was now considered the seat of the Anabaptist Movement in Brabant. Erasmus received a letter from a friend in Antwerp, saying, "We are in fear and anguish on account of these firebrands, the Anabaptists. There is scarcely a place or a town where the torch of revolt does not secretly glow. The communism which they preach attracts the masses far and wide."

However, the Anabaptists would have been no firebrands had they not been driven to desperation. In February, 1534, an Anabaptist apostle, Jan Joosten, a former priest, was put to death at Amsterdam for being a Baptist. His so-called confession, extracted by the rack, served as a starting-point of an extensive and thoroughly organized persecution. Bands of fifteen to twenty soldiers roamed the rural districts, accompanied by police officers, who arrested the suspected, generally coming on them at night and dragging them out of bed to prison. In Zwolle many hundreds were lying deprived of liberty, while in Utrecht about five hundred were in prison. Ships were also sent out to the Zuyder Zee, apparently to stop the Baptist vessels laden with emigrants. For the passage round the north of Holland to the mouth of the Ems was a comparatively easy way of reaching Münster.

In the beginning of 1534, a circular letter was spread throughout Holland, addressed to "all beloved companions in Christ," summoning them to come to Münster as to a new Jerusalem, for in that city were the signs of the Kingdom of God. They must fly out of Babylon and not look behind after unbelieving wife or child. On the 21st March, thirty ships filled with men, women, and children left Amsterdam, but none of them got farther than the entrance to Zwartsluis, in Overyssel. When those on board were asked whither they were going, they replied: "To the country that God shall show us." They were well provided with arms and were part of a great exodus out of Holland which, according to the magistrate at Grave, was to meet at Vollenhoven and was expected to number sixteen thousand persons. While this Anabaptist fleet was making its way to the trysting-place, multitudes of people were streaming thither from Gelderland and other parts of the Netherlands in wagons, on horses, and on foot. The authorities, on the alert, stopped and overpowered detachment after detachment and put the prisoners into jail. Then they scuttled five of the ships, drowning all on board. Of the prisoners taken, all the leaders were executed: their heads being stuck on poles, their bodies fastened to the wheel. The women and children were sent back to their homes. When the news arrived in Amsterdam, five Anabaptists, among them some who were apostles, went through the city, crying, "The blessing of the Lord hangs over one side of the city, the curse over the other," while one of them exclaimed, "The new city is given to the city of God. Woe, woe to all the wicked!" Possibly the people understood the allusions, but if it was a call to "awake, arise, or be forever fallen," they failed to respond.

On Christmas Day, 1534, there was a rising in Deventer, the object being to capture the city and use it for the advantage of the party at Münster, the first city of which the Baptists had got possession. As usual, the conspirators were betrayed, and the burgomaster's son, Jan van Winsum, and two others, were beheaded in the marketplace. At

Leiden, it was said, the Anabaptists had conspired to burn the city, and on January 25th, 1535, fifteen men and five women were arrested. The men were beheaded, the women drowned. Among the latter was, it is said, Jan Beukelsz'[2] wife, her crime being that she was not only an Anabaptist but had received Anabaptists into her house. On February 11th, according to the generally received account, some Anabaptists having met at a house in Amsterdam, at the call of one named Richard, they stripped themselves of their clothes and ran through the streets crying, "Woe! Woe! Woe! The wrath of God! The wrath of God!" Brought before the magistrates, they refused to dress. "We," they said, "are the naked truth." Their behavior on the scaffold gives reason to suppose that it was elevation of soul, rather than any other reason, which led them to this fanatical act. The woman at whose house this testimony began was hanged at her own door. In Hoorn, during the month of March, five persons were beheaded and two women were thrown into the sea. These executions excited so much compassion that the people of Hoorn determined to have no more fellow citizens put to death on account of religion.

Jan van Geelen, who had been sent from Münster, apparently to bring in fugitives, was in Friesland leading three hundred men, women, and children. Pursued by a troop, they entrenched themselves in a place called Olde-klooster, not far from Witmarssum, where Menno Simons dwelt. After struggling bravely for many days, they were overwhelmed by the soldiers. Most fell fighting. Of those who remained, the men were beheaded, and the women drowned. Menno's brother was among the slain. This happened on February 28th, 1535. Van Geelen escaped and reached Amsterdam. In May, the burgomaster learned that van Geelen entertained the idea of taking the city by surprise. While the magistrates were discussing what they should do, the Anabaptists attacked the Stadthuis. Some burghers, however, were aroused and came to the help of the authorities. The insurrectionists fired into the rescue party and killed one of the burgomasters. The other, sheltering his men with

2. Commonly called Jan van Leiden.

sails and hopsacks and inducing some volunteers to assist by the promise
of a month's pay, made an onset. But it was not until the morning,
when they brought cannons onto the Dam, the great space in front
of the Stadthuis, that they succeeded in wresting the building out of
the hands of the insurgents. The Anabaptists were only twenty-five in
number, but they fought like lions, yielding at last to the inevitable; for
the besiegers surrounded them on all sides, getting ladders and entering
through the windows of the Stadthuis. Twelve were finally taken alive
and were publicly executed on May 14th, in the brutal manner usual in
cases of treason. The dead bodies of those killed in the fight were hung
by their feet on the gallows. Jan van Geelen, flying up to the tower, was
shot.

Others connected with the outbreak—men and women—were subsequently executed. A widow and her son were drowned for harboring
the bishop of the Baptist community, Jan van Kampen.[3] He was found
hidden under some turf, was racked, and, with a two-cornered mitre
on his head, exposed to public derision. His tongue was then cut out
and thrown to the dogs, and the hand with which he had baptized was
cut off; next he was bound to a butcher's block and his head hacked off
with a cleaver; and finally, his body was burnt in the market. The con-
tingents from various places, which were to have helped in van Geelen's
enterprise, now arrived, but found themselves too late. Some escaped to
England.

4

On the 10th of June the Emperor and his council sanctioned a decree by
which all persons in the Netherlands, from Lille to Friesland, infected by
Anabaptism, with their abettors, followers, and accomplices, were liable
to forfeit their lives and goods. Prophets, apostles, bishops, baptizers,
were to be burnt to death. The rest, if they renounced their evil opinions,

---

3. Jan van Kampen is one whose life's story, as related by his enemies,
   is much bespattered. I regard the whole story with doubt.

and sincerely repented, were to suffer, the men with the sword, the women in a sunken pit—that is, they were to be buried alive.[4]

The reign of terror now set in. People were being put to death for Anabaptism everywhere. There were, during 1535, executions for Anabaptism in twenty-three towns in Holland, and little trouble was taken as to whether those who suffered were insurrectionists or not. No doubt there were two kinds of Anabaptists in the Netherlands. Some, as the first Baptists, believed in the doctrine of non-resistance to evil, sure that suffering was the only true method of Christian overcoming; but the great majority had entirely gone over to the new teaching of the prophet Matthysz. The former did not deny that the latter were their brothers, or that they sympathized with the great cause for which the militant party drew their swords. No separation can be made until after the fall of Münster.[5] The ground of the essential unity of all kinds of Anabaptists cannot be understood if looked at from a merely ecclesiastical point of view. The thought that the Kingdom of Heaven, of which the Gospels spoke, could be, and must be, realized on earth—this was the keynote that had brought into harmony the universal Anabaptist soul. And that soul is mirrored in hers who, in the moment of exultation, uttered the best-beloved of all the psalms of Christendom—the hymn of the poor, crushed peoples of the world, finally avenged and triumphant. That God would scatter the proud in the imagination of their hearts, that He would put down the mighty from their seats and exalt them of low degree, that He would fill the hungry with good things and send the rich empty away—this was the ardent desire of thousands and tens of thousands of hearts throughout Christendom, who, whether they believed in drawing the sword or not, wished well to the Anabaptist cause; for this meant to every Anabaptist a great deal more than being rebaptized on a profession of faith.

---

4. C. M, Davies' History of Holland, Vol. 1, p. 883.

5. Hoekstra, p. 16.

As the first Swiss Anabaptists regarded Münzer as their "dear brother Thoman," though he had not submitted to believers' baptism himself or given up baptizing children, though he used the Missal in public worship, and had no scruple about drawing the sword on behalf of the oppressed; so now, at this crisis, the Anabaptists of the Netherlands asked not if a man or woman regarded Battler or Denck, Hubmaier or Huter, Hoffmann or Matthysz, as his or her teacher. They did not, in fact, even make a difficulty of their being still in some outward connection with the Zwinglian, Lutheran, or Catholic churches. It was enough if they felt and acted as if the prophetic soul of the humble Virgin Mother lived again in them.

Yet, undoubtedly, the movement Matthysz had commenced, and which was now developing in a manner so astonishing at Münster, caused great searchings of heart. The vast majority of the anabaptistically inclined in the Netherlands threw themselves heart and soul into the movement and were preparing, like the children of Israel on the night of the first Passover, to leave the fleshpots of Egypt and to face all the terrors of the Red Sea and the wilderness in order to get to the Promised Land. But there were some few who suffered an inward agony as they saw that the new means taken to bring about the Kingdom of Justice and Peace were not its means, but such as would produce still greater injustice and more cruel strife. The position of these men and women was at this time terrible. On the one hand, the cause to which they had given themselves was the most sacred on earth. To quit it was to be another Judas Iscariot. Yet it was being dragged on to fearful disaster, and they knew themselves helpless to prevent it. Ubbo Philipsz has graphically described the position. He stood very near to Matthysz, having been baptized, as was his brother Dirk, by the apostles Matthysz sent out. He had further been ordained by these very apostles, Boeckbinder and Kuyper, a bishop of a Baptist community; and he had ordained as pastors in various places Menno Simons, David Joris, and his own brother Dirk. Thus he stood very close to the source of the new impulse. Yet, with the faithfulness to conscientious conviction so characteristic of these early Baptists, militant or not, he found himself obliged to oppose, on a crucial point, the men whom he no doubt had believed to be sent of God to bring him into the truth.

"God knows," he said, "that Dierick and I could not find it in our hearts to believe such a design (he means clearing the way for the righteous Kingdom by force) to be right but steadily taught the opposite. We knew not what to do. The whole world persecuted us for our faith with fire, water, sword, and every kind of bloody tyranny; the prophets deceived us from all quarters, and the letters written to us brought us to prison. The false brethren (the followers of Matthysz) whom we punished and opposed, swore death to us, and we had to bewail the lost love of so many hearts, that the most high King of Glory knows my soul was many times afflicted to death. There was a long time when no one among the teachers helped me. The false brothers stood up with much uproar against Dierick Philipsz."

These statements were made apparently some time later, when from the course of events Ubbo Philipsz began to take a worse and worse view of the matter and expressed himself accordingly. In any case, all he has said clearly proves that at that time no distinction had been drawn between the two sorts of Anabaptists, and that the vast mass of Baptists sympathized heartily with the movement now commencing in Münster.

Titles of Works Consulted

- Ten Cate, S. B.: *Geschiedenis der Doopsgezinden in Holland, Zeeland, Utrecht en Gelderland.*

- Ten Cate, S. B.: *Geschiedenis der Doopsgezinden in Friesland.*

- Müller, J.P.: *Die Mennoniten in Ostfriesland.*

- Brons, A.: *Ursprung, etc., der Taufgesinnten oder Mennoniten.*

- Hoekstra, S.: *Beginselen en Leer der Oude Doopsgezinden.*

- Van Braght: *Het Bloedig Tooneel, etc.*

- Underhill, E. B.: *Martyrology.*

6

Anabaptism in Northwestern Germany

1

Northwestern Germany, though divided into many States, had a common life, especially manifest at this time in its view of the Reformation, which it understood meant social and political, as well as religious, reform. Several of the States in this part of Germany had bishops for their sovereigns. In such States the root of power was the chapter of the diocese; and the chapter, with its rich canonries and prebends, was the appanage of the local aristocracy. Thus, in reality, the prince-bishop, being elected by the chapter, was the nominee of the aristocracy; and the two orders of clergy and knighthood, possessing also supremacy in the local diet, could generally defy the wishes of the people. By the combination of the governing classes in the various States this strong position was further strengthened; and thus it came to pass that in the episcopal States a few aristocratic families obtained hereditary power over the people, the result being that of the wealth and honour of the communities they controlled, the lion's share was theirs. The clergy especially, by the innumerable exemptions and immunities they obtained, made the burden of taxation heavier on the people, already depressed by a system which enabled the few to absorb the wealth made by the many. The cynical selfishness of those in power is shown by the fact that Bishop Frederic von Wied sold the diocese of Münster in 1532 to Eric, Duke and Bishop of Brunswick and Bishop of Paderborn, for forty thousand florins; and Eric's successor at Münster, Bishop Franz von Waldeck, entered in 1533, together with the chapter of Münster, into negotiations with the Burgundian Government for the sale of all the princely rights over the metropolis of the diocese: the sum offered for the sovereignty over the city of Münster being ten thousand crowns.

This Chapter, otherwise called "The Forty," from the number who composed it, elected the bishop, and was the leading power in the diocese. Only the very cream of the Münster aristocracy could gain admission into "The Forty"—at least four quarterings on their coats of arms were required. The inhabitants of Münster were divided into two castes—the ecclesiastical and the laical—the latter of whom bore the real burdens of the State. How numerous was the former caste appears from the fact that there were within the walls of Münster four other ecclesiastical foundations besides the Cathedral chapter, four monasteries, and seven nunneries, and ten churches in addition to the great Dom, or Cathedral. There were also four schools. So that Münster must have had about thirty ecclesiastical centers; which fact gives us some idea of the army of clericals the city contained, and suggests how large must have been the general population.

The ecclesiastical caste, notwithstanding its exclusive enjoyment of what belonged to the whole Christian church in Münster—that is, to the baptized community, which at that time meant everyone—entered into various trades and handicrafts, and even raised and sold cattle; thus competing with the artisans and tradespeople, a proceeding which was universally felt to be unfair. However, Kerssenbroick states that the Münster spirituality, by which he means the ecclesiastical caste, was so exemplary that it raised the holiness of the laity to a height equally edifying. "Such," he says, "was the chasteness, temperance, and moderation which adorned the spirituality that one would have declared that angels had taken human form, or men angels' manners." This dream, that Münster was an earthly paradise before the Anabaptist leaven began to work, fades away when we find that as early as 1523–24 the people had already accused the clergy to the Council of conduct rather more human than angelic. In a document they presented, containing their grievances in thirty-four articles, the eighteenth was as follows: "All unchaste females and the concubines of the priests shall be distinguished from spinsters of good repute by a certain sign, in order that the latter may receive due honor and the former be covered with shame."

A new conscience, in fact, awoke in Münster during the third decade of the sixteenth century, and some of the clerics were among the first to show signs of being affected by it. In four of the churches, the parsons, who had hitherto taught in an "irreproachable manner"—that is, in the conventional manner—began in 1522 to preach against the clergy and the authorities in the "rebellious tone" of the people. What that tone was we may judge from the way Kerssenbroick says some leader addressed the crowd in the street. "Why are you so sluggish? Do you not know that we shall soon possess freedom, that noble jewel which by nature all long after? Have you not heard that the dark reign of error is passing away—that the light of the Gospel, which until now has been obscured by the arrogance and selfishness of the Papists, is now spreading through the world—that their cheats have been discovered—that we are being delivered from this oppressive 'good works' yoke, and that evangelical freedom has made an end of the servitude every rational being must abominate?"

With the failure of the Peasant Insurrection in 1525, the efforts of the people in Münster to throw off the clerical yoke completely broke down, and things reverted to their old condition. In fact, after that great defeat of the cause of the people, all idea in Germany of attempting any serious reforms, economical or social, or of trying to ameliorate the condition of the poor, came to an end; on the contrary, the evils under which the poor suffered seem to have doubled. Things grew dearer, monopoly more grasping, the commercial companies battened on the people just as formerly, and capital for the first time began to show the full meaning of its powers.

Upon this depressing state of things came pestilence, famine, war. During the harvest of 1529, the Black Death, or sweating sickness, devastated Westphalia. Out of 500 struck with the plague in Dortmund, 470 died during the first four days. On the first evening it reached Minden, thirty fell sick and twenty were dead in the morning. In addition a famine set in so severe that there were places where the bushel of rye, which in the summer of 1529 cost three and a half shillings, rose during the next

summer to nine shillings. In Dortmund, where in 1530 it was five and
a half shillings, in 1531 it rose to fourteen shillings. In the same year an
extraordinary war tax was levied throughout the empire, on account of
the Turkish invasion; in the Cleve lands and some parts of Westphalia
it was extremely heavy. An archdeacon in Dortmund, writing in 1531,
speaks of the distress in that neighborhood as indescribable. With one
exception the authorities did not attempt to help the sufferers, who,
being left to choose between starvation and insurrection, frequently
tried the latter.

According to Melancthon, the struggle going on at this time in the
German cities was not so much on account of religion as for power and
freedom. But people always accustomed to the union of Church and
State might naturally think it part of religion to make the world's affairs
go on more justly, even though that meant getting rid of those who
considered its government their own hereditary possession. And this,
indeed, was exactly what the burghers in many of the cities in Northwestern Germany wished to effect. Both at Münster and at Osnabrück
the People, in 1525, rose and put forward their demands in a series of
articles. There were also unsuccessful popular movements at Minden
and at Paderborn. The latter city was forced by the bishop to pay a fine of
2,000 guilders, to agree to the clergy carrying on secular trades, to leave
all the privileges of the Chapter intact, and to put down all tendencies
to Lutheranism: a striking proof of the unity at this time of the three
movements for social, political, and religious reform.

The social point—the carrying on of secular trades by the clergy—was everywhere objected to, and one result of the popular defeat in
Münster was that the bishop forced the burghers of Münster to return
all the tools they had taken from the monasteries—that is to say, to
allow a number of rich communities of celibates, free from nearly all
the burdens and responsibilities of life, to enter into trade competition
with citizens who had families to maintain, taxes to pay, military service
to perform or provide, and who were not allowed to work except under
the stringent regulations of their guilds. And the Diet, in which the two
orders overbore the third estate, confirmed the clerical victory. Thus the
People everywhere saw no hope except in a complete reformation, and

they supported more or less vigorously every effort, social, political, or religious, which seemed likely to effect that end.

And this explains how it was that the social and political leaders of the time were so often ardent religious reformers and preachers of the Gospel. Bernard Rothmann, the name most associated with the struggle of the Münster democracy, is first heard of at the church of St. Mauritz, preaching the doctrine "that the true service of God consists in firm faith in Christ and in love to one's neighbor, rather than in fulfilling church ritual, fasting, mass-hearing, etc." Sympathetic and eloquent—from month to month, from day to day—Rothmann reflected the mood of the People. The monks of St. Mauritz shut him out of their church: he preached in the churchyard. The bishop inhibited him from preaching: he went on. The Chapter sought the intervention of the Emperor, but Rothmann, strong in the support of the People, remained at his post. Democracy in Münster had, in fact, a more than usually strong position, the Trade Guilds standing on the same ground as all the other existing powers; and through them, the people exercised a legally recognized influence, so that nothing very important could be done without the concurrence of their leaders, who met at the Schusterhaus (Shoemakers' Hall), or "Schauhaus," as it seems to have been called. Bernard Knipperdolling, the furrier who went with Hoffmann to Sweden, was the leader of the Münster democracy. He was a good speaker, prompt in action, and much respected. The Lutheran party, which had the support of several of the most intelligent members of the governing classes in Münster, was at this time so identified with the popular party that the growth of the power of the guilds increased in proportion to the growth of the evangelical faith in the city. Thus, the Shoemakers' Hall became a formidable rival to the Council House. The democracy, or people, of Münster already had friends in the latter, and they had only to wait for one or two more elections to get the government of Münster into their own hands.

By February 1532, the Evangelical movement in Münster had obtained such an amount of recognition from the authorities that its preachers delivered their first public sermons in the city in St. Lambert's churchyard—a true forum, for it was in the great marketplace of Münster. Rothmann was erelong appointed preacher at St. Lambert's. But the duke-bishop Eric, who had bought the diocese and sovereignty of Münster, came into possession on March 27th, 1532, and his first act was to require the removal of the new clergy, and Rothmann was ordered provisionally to suspend his preaching. This brought up the question, who ought to appoint the preachers—the Council or the Community? The preachers and their friends, being of opinion that right of appointment belonged to the Community, determined to refuse obedience to this order. The death of the new bishop, after a short reign of forty-eight days, probably rendered this decision more easy.

On the first of July a committee was appointed by the Evangelicals to bring things to a settlement with the Council, and by covenants on July 15th and August 10th the whole of the parish churches in Münster were made over to the evangelical clergy. This arrangement, however, needed the sanction of the new prince-bishop, Franz von Waldeck; and this, it was certain, he would not give, for an imperial mandate of July 12th required him to dismiss and expel the Lutheran ministers from Münster and to establish military order in the city. Therefore Münster does not appear to have asked the bishop's consent, but simply went on, avowing itself willing to give up liberty and life rather than the Word of God.

The bishop, in agreement with the civil and spiritual aristocracy, now decided to employ force. But the burghers showing a disposition to resist, and the bishop having no money, and being besides desirous to keep on good terms with his Lutheran neighbors, nothing came of his decision. Numbers of the spiritual and temporal aristocracy accordingly fled in alarm to Telgte, a short distance from Münster; but the place not being well fortified, 1,000 Münster men marched there one winter's night in 1532, and capturing the assembled nobles, landowners, and ecclesiastics, brought them back in triumph to Münster. The bishop himself only escaped by having the night before left the city. Under these circumstances, he accepted the mediation of Philip of Hesse and proclaimed a truce throughout the whole diocese. The condition of things agreed upon between the Council and the Lutheran leaders on August 10th, 1532, was now accepted by the bishop, chapter, and knighthood of the diocese and duly ratified by a treaty on February 14th, 1533. Thus, Münster became a Lutheran city.

2

The struggle in Münster was only part of a great movement going on, not only in the towns of that diocese but also in those of the neighboring states. The course it took at Warendorf is somewhat typical: image-breaking, demonstrations for the release of arrested monks, nomination of a committee to deal with the Council, seizure of a portion of the monastic wealth, establishment of Lutheranism, the revolution culminating in triumphant singing of German hymns in the great church.

With scarcely an exception, the Westphalian cities at this time not only became Lutheran but advanced in a social-democratic direction. The evangelical faith, as Luther first conceived it, was a really social-democratic faith. In Luther's doctrine of justification, there was no room for the aristocratic idea: the most wealthy morally must take the same place as the morally bankrupt. At the same time, Luther proclaimed a spiritual communism so complete and so profound that in its presence no opposing thought can stand. "Say to Christ," said Luther, "All that is Thine is mine, and all that is mine is Thine."

What prevented this great evangelical principle from being received as the social law which should govern the relations of men to each other was that those who preached it did not understand that it was the expression of the universal law by which we all live on one another. The preachers did not see that the misery of this world arises from men being subject to this law without understanding how to turn its curses into blessings. Luther had the key, but apparently did not know how to use it, for instead of opening the door, he set himself to put up again the bolts and bars which he had begun to take down.

In his earlier view of the church, he left all authority in the hands of the Christian community. It was to be the judge of doctrine, to call out ministers of the Word, and to appoint the deacons who were to preside over and administer its secular affairs. It was, in fact, a self-governing spiritual republic, dependent on no external spiritual authority.

But when Luther's opinions took a reactionary turn after 1525, the community was put in the background, and the power that he had considered inherent in it was handed over to the secular authorities. Henceforth, the preacher held his authority from the superintendent, and the superintendent received the commands of the ducal court or the civic magistrates.

Thus the people soon began to feel that Lutheranism had deceived them; that it had, in fact, made a treaty with the foe. Its power to console and inspire was gone; they saw their chains had been forged anew, and in the bitterness of their soul, they exclaimed, "To your tents, O Israel; now see to thine own house, David."

It is certain that after the great defeat of the People in 1525, many thousands who until then had been Lutherans went over to the Baptists. Sebastian Franck says, speaking of this time, "The Baptist movement was so swift that their doctrine soon spread over the whole country, and they soon baptized many thousands, many excellent people being drawn to them." Luther's attitude towards the great social-democratic movement of his time is the explanation.

When the medieval church was given up in Münster, it was intended to set up a Lutheran church in its place, and Rothmann was entrusted with the preparation of its constitution and order. Beyond the election of preachers and one or two other matters, Rothmann's plans never came into existence. The cause of this was the now rapid development in Münster of the People's idea of the Reformation.

3

As already stated,[1] the effect of the new ecclesiastical establishment in Cleve was so inimical to the religious work of the Wassenberg preachers that Roll, Vinnen, Kloprys, the bailiff of Wassenberg, Staprade, and Slachtscaep all sought a refuge in Münster. It proved a momentous decision, both for themselves and for that city. They were not only heartily

---

1. Refer to p. 6.

welcomed, but in the course of time, several of them became preachers under the new ecclesiastical arrangements, their views harmonizing with the point at which public opinion had arrived in Münster. Roll had been their teacher, and his large-hearted, large-minded way of thinking brought these ministers into complete unity. Into their company, Rothmann first and then Stralen, another of the Lutheran clergymen of the city, entered; and in the midst of the terrible trials they had to go through, these preachers kept in such accord and brotherhood, that never on any occasion do we hear of the slightest difference of opinion between them. Roll's views on the sacraments soon became those of Rothmann and of Münster. Roll, as already said, regarded the Lord's Supper as a memorial feast and a witness to the central fact of the Gospel, while he rejected infant baptism altogether. The prevalence of these views soon caused trouble, for they interfered with the policy of the chief politician in Münster, the Syndic Van der Wieck. His aim was to bring about a union between the Lutheran cities of Northwestern Germany. When, therefore, he found that the city he represented was being drawn away from a Lutheran to an Anabaptist basis, he set himself determinedly to prevent it. This was not easy, as the new Council elected on the 3rd of March, 1533, was mainly formed of men belonging to the democratic party. However, the Syndic's representations of the position Münster would be in, if the city undertook to defy the Empire, had some effect.

Rothmann, worked upon by his sister and her husband, the Lutheran preacher Brixius, as well as by some of his old Lutheran friends in the Council, promised to refrain from any further attacks on infant baptism. It is evident, however, that he saw that he would be carried along in spite of his promises, for when his sister adjured him, with tears, not to bring the city and himself to ruin, he replied, "That may be as it may; I am bound to go forward." The popular movement was in truth no isolated one, but extended to all parts of Germany. Wherever there had been an insurrectionary center in the time of the Peasant War, there, in all probability, the democracy of Münster had sympathizers; and now the undefeated and vigorous populations of the Dutch Netherlands and Northern Germany were waking up to the importance of the crisis and were beginning to work for the overthrow of the oligarchies in power.

Rothmann's promises evidently bound no one but himself; for Staprade, his coadjutor at St. Lambert's, was now accused of saying that the baptism of infants was an abomination before God. To show the people of Münster that all evangelical Germany was against their preachers, the Council sought outside aid. Melanchthon wrote to Rothmann, Urban Rhegius to the Council, and Marburg University sent a judgment adverse to the Wassenberg doctrine on the Church and the sacraments. Van der Wieck also worked to combine into one party all the Lutherans, Zwinglians, and Catholics in Münster on the common ground of resistance to the radical tendencies of the preachers and the people.

Those who had not been prominent were now evidently forced to declare themselves; and when the Lutheran preacher Stralen went over to the side of the people, the democratic party had possession of nearly all the pulpits in Münster.

Van der Wieck, driven to his wits' end, now tried the usual resort of the Reformers before finally crushing their opponents. He arranged a disputation, which took place on the 7th and 8th of August, 1533. It appears to have turned chiefly on the views of Roll and Staprade upon infant baptism.

Herman van den Bossche, supported by the preachers Wertheim and Brixius, together with two evangelical laymen and two friars, appeared on one side; Rothmann and the Wassenberg preachers on the other. Rothmann won an easy victory, for Van den Bossche, pleading age and ill health, did not reply. The result was embarrassing for the Council. However, they acted as if their champion had won, and ordered the preachers to administer infant baptism.

On September 7th, 1533, some councillors brought their children to St. Lambert's and requested Staprade to baptize them. He refused, and, being accused to the Council, was ordered to quit the city. The rest of the preachers were then summoned to appear and peremptorily required to baptize the children under pain of being deprived of their office. Rothmann, Stralen, Roll, Kloprys, and Vinnen distinctly refused obedience (September 17th). It was, they said, an usurpation for the civil authorities to interfere in such matters; if they had anything against the preachers, they must make their accusation in the assembly of the believers.

The Council closed the churches of the refractory preachers and deprived Rothmann of his office. The guilds, by their officials, intervened, and peace was made between Rothmann and the Council (October 3rd), the former undertaking not to raise the controverted points until "the Lord had given further intelligence and knowledge of the truth."

This strife filled the bishop and chapter with such hope that they gave up the idea of selling the civil dominion of Münster to the Burgundian Government. The Council, on the other hand, had so altered their views since they were elected six months earlier that they began to draw near to the bishop, who immediately tested the extent to which they would go by ordering a Catholic preacher to deliver a sermon in the Cathedral. Between the bishop and the people of Münster, the Council was in a great dilemma. They sent the Catholic preacher out of the city and tried to get the corporation of the guilds to support them in exiling Rothmann. When this was refused, the Council came to the desperate resolution to coalesce with their old enemies, the clerico-aristocratical party, who at once proposed to defend the Council with arms— that is to say, to commence a civil war with a view to crush the People. Van der Wieck energetically repelled the idea, but this awakening of the hopes of those who deemed themselves robbed of their hereditary right to rule Münster did, in a very short time, bring the city to the condition of civil war. After a night under arms (November 6th), peace was brought about by the Wassenberg preachers agreeing to quit the city. Rothmann remained but still deprived of his office.

The Council, now in possession of the field, attempted, with the aid of two preachers sent by Philip of Hesse, to set up a State church in Münster, but their efforts were not successful. Van der Wieck appears to have considered Rothmann's presence the cause and, conceiving his actions to spring from vanity, suggested to the Landgrave that he should, by special messengers, invite "the viper" to his court. But Rothmann had no intention of separating his fate from that of Münster, gloomy as were his forebodings. One of his former friends came to Münster and was offered a preachership by the Council. Before accepting, he sought an interview with Rothmann, which the latter avoided. One day, however, the prospective preacher's wife met Rothmann in the street and spoke to him of her husband. "My sister," he said, "let him go where the people have given him a call; things will not turn out well here."

The state of things in Münster strengthened the clerico-aristocratical party in other parts of the diocese. The bishop suddenly appeared at Dulmen, a town a few miles from Münster, with a mounted troop and clapped the leaders of the evangelical party into prison, together with some preachers from Münster. In Warendorf, a popular movement was put down, while at Alen, the exiled priests and banished nobles suddenly carried off the cattle of the inhabitants. These proceedings produced a panic among the evangelicals in the diocese, and reaction set in at Dulmen, Warendorf, Coisfeld, and Beckum, extending to the neighboring diocese of Osnabrück.

4

While these social and political struggles were in progress, the Hoffmannite form of Anabaptism rapidly spread over Northwestern Germany and the northern Netherlands. Its preachers came to Münster and openly preached in the marketplace. Rothmann, who in 1532 had warned the people against Hoffmann, was now reading his writings, and Roll was doing the same. The restraint which Hoffmann had put on the practice of baptism for two years favored the progress of his ideas among those disposed to listen to his prophetical expositions but not prepared to profess themselves Baptists. By the end of 1533, Hoffmann's views prevailed generally among the Baptists of the northwestern portion of the empire.

Meanwhile, the Münster preachers—Rothmann, Kloprys, Staprade, Roll, Vinnen, and Stralen—had issued, in November of the same year, their "Confession on both Sacraments," which shows that by the autumn of 1533, every one of them, and without doubt a great number of their followers, had become Baptists in principle. Kerssenbroick represents Rothmann as going by night to Anabaptist conventicles in Münster, where laymen discoursed on the main points of the Baptist faith. The followers of Rothmann were at this time, as was their leader, distinguished for earnestness and self-sacrificing devotion. They sought to exemplify equality and brotherhood in their lives. Well-to-do Brothers and Sisters gave all their goods to the poor, destroyed their rent-rolls, forgave their debtors, renounced worldly pleasures, studying to live an unworldly life. Among such was Knipperdolling's mother-in-law, who was very rich.

The "Confession on both Sacraments" described baptism as "a dipping or plunging completely into water, for only under this form can it be spoken of as being buried with Christ. But this putting of the body into water is of little use to the soul if the baptized deny their ability to be good, to lay aside the desire to sin, resolving henceforth to give willing obedience to Christ; for this is the salvation to be aimed at, and this it is which is required in baptism. Those who are baptized, through their confession of faith and in the power of faith, lay aside the entire old life and henceforth by their walk through life deny that old life; in this way, indeed, (water) baptism becomes the beginning of another baptism, which with sure knowledge directs the conscience, renewed and born again through the Holy Ghost, to forsake and die to all unrighteousness and all works of darkness."[2]

Baptism, the Confession further said, "is a gate or entrance into the Holy Church and a following after Jesus Christ. But to make baptism a vehicle of grace agrees with no scripture. Plunging into water is only an outward sign, and an outward sign is not always what it professes to be." "Baptism does not depend for its efficiency on the act itself or on the words spoken or on the faith of the father or on unrequired vows or sureties or on citizenship, but rather on this: that the baptized, through his own knowledge of Christ, his own faith, gives up his sinful lusts and offers himself to Christ. This, in short, is our understanding of what baptism is and how it is to be made use of."

This Confession served as a manifesto to the friends of the Anabaptist movement everywhere and was doubtless widely disseminated by

---

2. Bouterwek I Literatur und Geschichte der Wiedertäufer, p. 7.

its emissaries. For from the beginning, the spirit of Anabaptism was essentially missionary. Matthysz' first act was to send out apostles, and the Anabaptist Community at Münster did the same both in February and in October 1534.

5

In following the traces of Anabaptism in various cities and towns from the Meuse to the Baltic, we gain some idea of the extent to which the Baptist propaganda succeeded and better understand the import of the struggle now opening up in Münster. At Liege and Maestricht, there were Baptist communities organized on the South German model, and at the latter place, Roll, by this time a Baptist in fact as well as in principle, was working in 1534. Both towns were in close union with Aix-la-Chapelle, the three forming an equilateral triangle, and here, it appears, was another community in connection with those of Liege and Maestricht. There was also a community at Susteren, on the road between Maestricht and Wesel. From Aix-la-Chapelle to Cologne, the road is direct, and at Cologne, there was a community of 700 members. Dr. Gerard Westerburg, brother-in-law of Carlstad, is said to have introduced Anabaptism into Cologne in 1530, although he and his brother Arnold were themselves baptized in Knipperdolling's house as late as 1534. Westerburg returned to Cologne, where his abode became the meeting place of the Baptist community, and there also new members were baptized. A letter written by Archbishop Hermann, expressing fear lest the rebellious enterprises of the Anabaptists should lead to a rising of the "Common Man," was followed by executions in November 1534 in Cologne. Richard, a glassmaker, was burnt, and two others were beheaded.

Maestricht was a center from which Roll could act on his old friends in the Wassenberg district. Slachtscaep, Kloprys, Staprade were all in these parts laboring to strengthen the cause. In connection with Jacob of Osnabrück's apostolate, we hear of a meeting at which thirty-eight journeymen decide to start for Münster. They go by boat from Neuss to Düsseldorf, where they are stopped and imprisoned. At Wesel, where

Roll began baptizing, Otto Vinck and Wilhelm Schlebuss, both high in office in the city, submitted to the rite, the sympathies of the people being so strongly Anabaptist that the Cleve Chancellor already suspected the city of tending to union with Münster. Knipping, a saddler, was pointed out to the Cleve Government as the head of the movement.

The Cleve Government spread light cavalry over the country to prevent any gatherings, and after April 1534, produced a complete set of measures for suppressing any movement. Towards the end of 1534 (December 20th), the Duke of Cleve and the Archbishop of Cologne agreed together to carry out the imperial mandate, and to put to death all twice baptized persons, and all who despised infant baptism.

Meanwhile a movement analogous to that of Münster had been going on at Soest, then a flourishing and populous town, on the highway of commerce between the Netherlands and the Baltic. The struggle commenced between early democratic Lutheranism and the possessors of power, who remained Roman Catholic. But when Luther fell back from his original position, and to secure his reformation surrendered the management of the Church to the civil authorities, the evangelical party practically split up; those who followed Luther in his reaction tending to union with the old rulers and governing families, those who remained attached to Luther's original position becoming more and more democratic. These circumstances were favourable, as elsewhere, to the entry of Zwinglianism into Soest, and finally, under all this apparent religious and political confusion, it is evident the community was divided into two opposing sections: the rich and respectable, and the poor and discontented. The former were beaten at first by the overwhelming numbers and energy of the people; but by a federation of all the various authorities and their dependents, closely bound together by an oath, and by terror—striking, ruthless acts, they managed to overawe the Soest democracy. The struggle had reached this stage of popular depression and embitterment when Soest was, in 1534, visited by Anabaptist apostles. In the spring of that year Johann of Warendorf, an apostle from Münster, came to Soest, several persons getting into trouble with reference to his visit. In October, 1534, eight apostles arrived from Münster, among them the prophet Dusentschur and the Wassenberg preacher

Slachtscaep. They were arrested on October 21st, and on the 23rd were sentenced to death and immediately executed.

In May, 1534, Duke Ernest of Lüneburg wrote that the whole bishopric of Münster and the surrounding land were infected with Anabaptism. From the judicial examination of Jurgen Wullenweber, the fallen burgomaster of Lübeck, it appears that the whole of Northwestern Germany was inclined to Anabaptism—the people no doubt sincerely, many influential personages for personal and political ends. The leaders dared not go far enough and so could not arouse the people to sufficient enthusiasm. According to Wullenweber, the various towns in Northwestern Germany were only waiting for each other to declare themselves Baptist. Lübeck was one of the four Hanse centers of Germany, and such was its wealth and power in the middle of the fifteenth century that Aeneas Sylvius (Pius II) writes in 1458, "Denmark, Sweden, and Norway are accustomed to elect and depose kings at a sign from Lübeck." So at this time Wullenweber said, "If Lübeck went Baptist, Hamburg would; and to induce Lübeck to take the lead they worked for Bremen to come in. If Lübeck went Baptist, the change would be carried out in Brunswick, the Hanse center in Saxony; and the burgomaster of Brunswick believed that on Lübeck's action that of Hannover and Magdeburg depended." In the spring of 1534, in some districts of the Münster diocese the peasants rose and determined to follow whatever was established at Lübeck and in the county of Holstein.

How Lübeck inclined appears from the fact that the democracy there refused to allow any decree against Anabaptism; that in the spring of 1534 a treaty was made between Lübeck and Münster; and that people on all hands were looking for Lübeck to take the lead. By 1533, the Anabaptists had become so powerful in Bremen that the city was within an ace of doing what Münster did in the following year. The Senate was compelled to withdraw from the city, and it was only after a severe struggle that peace was restored. But the people's heart was towards Anabaptism, and severe penalties were enacted against those who dared to scatter Anabaptist poison and to disseminate the writings and books from Münster and other places. Yet the Anabaptist fire went on burning in Bremen.

In Minden, Nicolaus Krage, the founder of the Lutheran Church there, tended to Anabaptism. In 1532, a democratic victory took place, and some working men were among the new councilors. Krage's sympathies were so much with the people that he lived among them in a village, outside the town, inhabited by fisherfolk. "Bethany, near Jerusalem," was the title he gave it. If he did not choose such bad company for base purposes, such sympathies proved him a dangerous man. So the Town Council determined in March 1535 to get rid of him. They closed the gates, collected a number of armed citizens, and marched on the village. They were received with shots and stones; however, they planted a cannon in front of the house where Krage lived and prepared to fire into it. The people's preacher gave himself up and was sent away from Minden.

The reformation in Osnabrück was led by Dietrich Buithmann; he and Dietrich of Mors, or Meurs, a Lutheran from Münster, were appointed as preachers in Osnabrück in 1532. A year later, Buithmann appears as a champion of the cause of the poorer part of the community. He and his colleague were banished. Anabaptist in spirit, if not in name, were these Lutheran preachers, and Osnabrück supplies at least three names recorded among those in Münster in 1534–35. In 1534, when apostles from Münster appeared there, they were given up to the bishop. We know not their fate, but can have little doubt what it was.

We now approach the towns nearest Münster. Warendorf, the largest, was evidently in sympathy with Münster, for several of its inhabitants transferred themselves thither as to the center of the struggle. An episcopal admonition was sent, but it received little attention; while the Münster apostles, who arrived on October 24th, 1534, were welcomed. Among them were Stralen, Rothmann's old colleague of Lutheran days, and Kloprys, the Wassenberg preacher. The bishop arrived with an army and soon took the city. The apostles and several citizens being brought before the bishop, Stralen and three others were publicly executed. Kloprys, as a subject of Cologne, was handed over to Archbishop Hermann, who burnt him on February 1st, 1535. The town of Warendorf was deprived of all its rights, freedoms, and privileges; all its arms were removed; a citadel was built at the cost of the town; all the councilors were put in prison, and an episcopal bailiff ruled the city, the keys being given up to the commander of the garrison.

At Coesfeld, another town near Münster, the Council at first refused to give up the eight apostles who had come to them; but, after seeing what had happened at Warendorf, they surrendered them to the bishop. In order to strike terror into the whole diocese the bishop led his captives to Horstmar, Borken, Vreden, Bocholt, and then put them to death on the wheel.

The villages and smaller towns round Münster had already been terrorized. In March, 1534, ten persons were arrested at Horstmar, and an executioner was sent on the 26th to carry out the sentences. At the little town of Wolbeck five were executed, and at Bevergern six persons were burnt alive. Thus the bishop, like some Spanish matador, flourished the blood-red flag in the eyes of the Münster Anabaptists.

Titles of Works Consulted

- Cornelius, C. A.: *Geschichte des Münsterischen Aufruhrs*.

- Keller, L.: *Geschichte der Wiedertäufer*.

- Janssen, J.: *Geschichte des Deutschen Volkes*.

- Bonerwek: *Zur Literatur und Geschichte der Wiedertäufer*.

7

The Anabaptist Kingdom in Münster

1[1]

Tortured on the rack, tortured in mind and spirit, compelled to betray friends they loved and the God on whom all their hopes were centered, scourged, imprisoned in foul dungeons, burnt to death in slow fires, beheaded, mutilated, their women drowned or put alive into coffins and strangled, the Anabaptist people of Germany and the Netherlands began to cry inwardly for vengeance, and to believe that their prayer was heard. And "the Common Man" sympathized with them, and they with "the Common Man," instinctively feeling that their enemies were one and the same—the rulers of this world. Brought by their banishment from Münster into closer contact with this double movement, how could the Wassenberg preachers help being dominated by its spirit? And that spirit was now again the spirit of Thomas Münzer. Nor could they, agreeing in all respects with the Anabaptists, fail to see their duty. Was not this very suffering the Divine token?

---

1. See the excursus at the end of this chapter for an explanation on the difficulty of sources on the following events.

Were not these the men who had the letter *Tau*[2] marked on their foreheads? They returned to Münster and threw in their lot with "the sect everywhere spoken against." On January 5th, 1534, two Hollanders arrived in Münster, apostles sent out by Jan Matthysz. That they used the words, "Repent, for the Kingdom of Heaven is at hand," that they denounced the wrath of God on all tyrants and bloodshedders, that they called on the believers in Münster to be baptized and form a true Community, in which all should be equal and have all things in common, can hardly be doubtful. Rothmann, Kloprys, Vinnen, and Stralen were baptized, and with Roll were appointed to baptize others. The rite was performed in Rothmann's house, and, judging from the terms of "the Confession," was probably by immersion. In eight days there were already 1,400 baptized persons in Münster.

Of their state of mind they have left this record: "In the day God awakened us so that we were faithful to be baptized, there was poured out a spirit, a brotherly love, rising to the flood tide." And of their consecration therein they say: "Whatever we now find day by day that God wills among us, that will we do, cost what it may."

On the 13th of January, two more apostles arrived, of whom one was Jan van Leiden, preaching a separation between the Church and the World, a separation which, among other things, called for a cessation of marriages between believers and unbelievers. On the 23rd, an edict came from the bishop, ordering the imprisonment and extradition of

---

2. In "The Restitution," written by Rothmann and Kloprys, and published a little later on, in speaking of those who had been awakened and appointed to execute vengeance upon the Heathen, it is said, "They are those who are marked with the mark Thau, concerning whom God said to the young man wearing the linen robe, with the inkhorn at his side (Ezekiel 9), 'Go through the streets of Jerusalem and mark a Thau (the last letter of the Hebrew alphabet, which in the most ancient writing had the form of a cross) upon the foreheads of the men who sigh and cry for all the abominations that be done in the midst thereof.'" See Bouterwek, p. 59.

all the Baptists in Münster. The answer was given at the next election for the Council when the Anabaptists were victorious, but meanwhile, a whole month elapsed during which great anxiety prevailed in the city. No one appears very prominently as the leader; each step seems to come from the People. The nunnery in the Oberwasser parish was a scene of commotion; nearly all the nuns came out and returned to ordinary life. Crowds pressed forward to be baptized, some bringing their possessions and giving them up to the Community. Women as well as men began to preach. These strange things were attributed by the aristocratic-clerical party to the sorcery of Rothmann, who, it was said, administered to all whom he baptized poisonous drugs from a wooden flask. But the People bewitched Rothmann, rather than Rothmann the People. One of those wonderful movements of the common soul had taken place, unaccountable on the theory that communities of men are but congregations of individual units.

At the sound of the voices of Jan van Leiden and Knipperdolling crying in the streets, "Repent!" the people hurry out of their houses and shops into the marketplace. Suddenly there is a great silence. Georg zum Berge, father of one of the prophetesses, with bare head and uplifted hand, is crying out, "You are looking, dear brothers, on your leaders. I see the glory of God in heaven, and Jesus carrying the flag of victory in His right hand. Woe to the wicked, who harden their hearts so obstinately. Repent! Repent!" And this is the conclusion of his sermon, "Leave now your wicked way, for the vengeance of God is at hand, and take upon you the sign of the new covenant." Then, springing to the ground, he prostrates himself in the form of a cross. Finally, he rises and goes to Knipperdolling's house. Young eyes that have been looking in the direction of the sky, to which the preacher's hand had pointed, now stare at the house into which he has entered. There Knipperdolling is seen with his face to the wall and his lips moving as if in prayer. In addition to scenes of this kind, there was continual alarm lest any night a struggle might break out, ending in a massacre. On the 7th of February, both sides were in arms; the Anabaptists gathered in the marketplace and about the Council house, while their opponents, who had seized Knipperdolling and the preachers Vinnen and Stralen, were in an entrenched position in the Oberwasser Church. Suddenly, the news arrived that the bishop was coming. The burgomaster, Tilbeck, hastened to patch up a peace, on the basis of an agreement on both sides to respect each other's religious liberty.

The aristocratic-clerical party now left the city, while Baptists from all parts began to come in, and among them men of position and wealth. The burgomaster, Tilbeck, proclaimed himself a Baptist, while the syndic, Van der Wieck, fled. He was arrested at Vecta, was brought to Furstenau, and there, without law or justice, was by order of the bishop beheaded.

2

The new Council, chosen on February 23rd, was Anabaptist, Knipperdolling and another Anabaptist, Kippenbroick of Amsterdam, being chosen burgomasters. Thus the Baptists won Münster, and that without any change in the constitution of the city. In the same month, the siege commenced, but, the bishop being without money, it went on very slowly. However, he took care, as already stated, to overawe the neighboring towns and villages by ruthless executions.

The victorious party in Münster now cleared the Dom, or cathedral, of all the objects they considered superstitious, their destructive zeal being specially exhibited against all deeds or documents which might contain abridgments of, or encroachments on, their liberties. Unfortunately, they destroyed at the same time many valuable books and works of art. This iconoclastic fury lasted a full week. As the city was being surrounded by episcopal forces, the new authorities determined that all the besiegers' friends must leave. The order, therefore, went out for all who were not Baptists to go; the greater part went, but some, like Gresbeck, preferred to commit sacrilege rather than lose hold on their property.

It was hard upon the expelled people, and we may suppose many of the Anabaptists felt a sad foreboding as they saw their unhappy neighbors forced to leave house and home. But the alternative was either this or worse severities; for suspected spies and traitors fare badly in war.

This explanation of the exodus of February 27th enables us to understand how it was that the religious leaders in Münster, to whom we must now add Jan Matthysz himself, considered it necessary that those among the recently baptized who bore arms should be made to feel the serious nature of the step they had taken. They were summoned into the marketplace, ordered to lay down their arms, and addressed on the necessity of repentance and faith. "God," they were told, "would not have the impure in the city, and only those who were converted would be allowed to remain." They prostrated themselves on their faces, according to the custom of the Baptists for penitential prayer, and were left in that position a long time. Then they were told to stand up, and were marched to St. Lambert's Church. Here they remained still longer, beseeching the divine mercy. Finally, Jan van Leiden appeared and, standing before the altar, declared that God's grace had reached them, and that they should remain in the city and be a holy people. After which, the converts passed in single file before Jan van Leiden and the preacher Slachtscaep, who, laying their hands on the head of each one, blessed them. The whole company then marched back to the marketplace and resumed their arms.

To comprehend what now went on in Münster, we must get as near as we possibly can to the point of view of the chief actors. Bunyan's "Holy War" will help us to do so. The firm conviction that this world is everywhere, and in every form of human life, individual or social, the scene of a struggle between the forces of good and evil, between the servants of Shaddai and the servants of Diabolus, possessed Bunyan as it did every true Anabaptist in Münster. Just as in Mansoul, after its conquest by Emmanuel, it became the first duty of its chief men to arrest every Diabolonian, to show him no mercy, but to put him speedily out of the way of doing any more harm; so now in Münster, this was the only treatment the dominant spirit thought fit for those who showed themselves opponents of the new kingdom of the saints.

An early and typical fact is the story of Hubert Ruscher, "the tall smith." Ruscher had a keen sense of his citizenship and could not tolerate the foreigners who were flocking into the city, and who, in the persons of Matthysz and Jan van Leiden, had almost gained the lordship. While on guard, he expressed his discontent to the rest of the watch. He was arrested, brought into the marketplace, and surrounded by a solemn circle of armed saints. He was adjudged guilty of death. According to the story, for reasons difficult to understand, the sentence, although attempted immediately, was not effectively carried out. Perhaps the protests that arose from some present paralyzed the efforts of Matthysz and Jan van Leiden, who acted as executioners.

The point, however, is not so much the barbarous manner in which the sentence was executed, as the fact that the penalty of death was exacted at all among a people who only a few years earlier had leaders opposed to all capital punishment, no doubt because they believed that every human body was a temple of God. Clearly, the theology prevalent in Münster was fundamentally different from that taught by Denck.

3

The feeling in Münster against the churches was such that the people no longer worshipped in them but always spoke of them as "the coldstone places." They preferred to unite in worship wherever the opportunity offered and when they felt moved to do so. Sometimes worship was held in the open air when the prophets preached; sometimes in smaller gatherings in houses, where the Scriptures were expounded and hymns sung. At other times, a general cessation of work was proclaimed, that the Community might celebrate the Lord's Supper. Then the people were exhorted to pardon all offenses and be reconciled to each other, and the Communion was held in certain houses in connection with an evening meal of the character of a love feast. Love feasts were also held in connection with the watch system at the city gates. While at these religious banquets those present ate and drank in a joyous manner, the preachers exhorted them to steadfastness and sincerity in faith. Then they pledged themselves to faithful comradeship and, singing a hymn, went to work.

The Council now resolved to establish community of goods as the new social order, and the people were invited to bring their gold and silver to the Council house, forgive each other their debts, and henceforth live as brothers and sisters. It was, however, two months before this communism actually became the rule in Münster. Three deacons were appointed in each parish to superintend the common provisions. They had to inquire what each house possessed, and those who had a superfluity were asked to give to those who were in want. Community houses were opened, at which there were common meals. In these houses preaching went on every day from morning till noon. Those who arranged the food were to give the same to each, and to each a separate plate. Stores of all kinds of food were collected and laid up for use. The various trades were organized, those specially mentioned being the fishmongers, butchers, grocers, confectioners, shoemakers, tailors, tanners, leather dressers, rape oil preparers, iron-workers, locksmiths, and horse doctors. Fish must not be refused the sick. Fresh meat must be ready at the appointed time. The smiths and iron-workers must only work for the authorities. No new fashions in dress were to be introduced, and no one was to go in torn or ragged garments. Wine and strong drinks were to be under special superintendence, and were to be used for the sick and those in great pain. The laborers on the public works were specially to be cared for—they would often need bread and beer. This practical ability and intelligent organization existed in combination with a state of mental fever, the result of the extraordinary circumstances of the time, and of the still more extraordinary ideas that had got possession of the Münster Anabaptists.

Hille Feiken, a young Friesland woman, like Charlotte Corday in later times, thought herself called upon to emulate Judith and to assassinate the man who played the part of Holofernes to the people of God. She was beautiful, talented, and, it is needless to add, full of devotion. She went alone out of the city into the besiegers' camp, and her intention being divulged by one who had escaped from the city, she was racked and beheaded. The Münster authorities, civil and religious, could have prevented Hille Feiken from attempting to carry out her design, but they did not. If they thought, as Jan van Leiden said, that it was "fantasy," they were to blame much more than Hille Feiken.

But they were themselves, and Jan van Leiden especially, in the same mental condition as Hille Feiken. Towards Palm Sunday, 1534, Jan was sitting in Knipperdolling's writing room, when he saw in a vision one come and run a weapon through Matthysz. Terrified at the sight, he heard a voice which said, "Why fear? that which I would have performed through Jan Matthysz, you shall now accomplish, and take his wife in marriage." He told Knipperdolling apparently the same day, but according to the latter, said nothing about Matthysz' wife. Perhaps Jan van Leiden felt it difficult, seeing that he was already married to Knipperdolling's stepdaughter.

Hardly a week had passed when, at a joyous festival held on Easter Saturday, April 4th, Matthysz suddenly exclaimed, "Dear Father, not as I will, but as Thou wilt." Then with hand and kiss he bade them all farewell. He must go out as Samson to defy the Philistines: he must lead a sortie against the besiegers.

Followed by about twenty devoted followers, he went out of the Ludgergate. A superior force of soldiers came to meet him. Meanwhile, the Münster people gathered on the walls, anxiously waiting for the outcome. They soon saw their champion surrounded by the enemy, and one after another of his followers fall. But for a long time, in the midst of the struggling mass, the prophet stood erect. At last, he also fell, and the soldiers descended upon him like a pack of hounds on a dying stag.

Thus, this stern figure, forerunner of Covenanter and Camisard, passed away, and his mantle fell on Jan van Leiden, who, calling the Community together, is reported to have said, "God has willed that Matthysz should die, lest we should believe too much in him. What this man did, God did through him and is able to give us another prophet even greater than he was." In a short time, Jan van Leiden was acknowledged as the prophet in the room of Matthysz.

The Anabaptist theocracy had its Moses and its Joshua; now it must have its Judges. Next, a Samuel will arise to whom the true David will be revealed. So now the new prophet announced that the Council was to be abolished, and in its place, twelve Elders were to rule the city according to a new law. The twelve Elders each received a drawn sword from the hands of Rothmann, who said, "Take herewith the power of life and death that by me God the Father confides to thee, and use this sword in conformity with His will."

The twelve Elders put forth a new law, in which the penalty of death was appointed for blasphemy, disobedience to, or contempt of, the Elders and Judges, unsubmissiveness to husbands, perverse, stubborn behaviour to masters, adultery, seduction, unchastity and the like, avarice, robbery, theft, fraud, overreaching, lying, scandal-mongering, shameful talk, enmity, hatred, envy, wrath, quarrelling, schism, faction, murder, tale-bearing and murmuring. But this Draconian code was, in point of fact, one of the mildest, for a clause remitted the penalty if the convicted person truly repented. By other ordinances the Elders were to walk twice a day to the judgment seat to settle all disputes; the prophet Jan was to proclaim the decision of the Elders; and Bernard Knipperdolling was appointed guardian of the public order and executor of the judicial sentences.

Marriage was a subject which much occupied the Reformers. Not only was there the great question of the celibacy of the clergy, but morals with relation to marriage had fallen in Germany to a low state at the close of the middle ages. Concubinage and adultery were everyday facts among the middle classes. The morals of the aristocracy may be judged by the fact that historians, wishful to throw a charitable veil over monastic and clerical corruption, admit the immorality of the nunneries exclusively occupied by noble-women. If we may trust the facts collected by Kriegk,[3] a condition of things existed in Germany towards the close of the fifteenth and the beginning of the sixteenth century which places this period among the most corrupt in history. The Anabaptist rulers had to deal with a population that had come out of such a state of things, a population now shut up as in a cage, and the proportion of women to men as two, or even as three to one. Of the unbaptized who still remained after the exodus of February 27th, the women were six to seven times as numerous as the men. How was the New Jerusalem to be

---

3. Kriegk: Deutsches Bürgerthum im Mittelalter.

preserved from becoming morally worse than Augsburg or Cologne?[4] The way of escape seemed to open in the fundamental thought of Münster Anabaptism—the restitution or restoration of all things according to the pattern of Holy Scripture. Now marriage in the Bible, especially in its earlier conditions, was polygamous. All the patriarchs had more than one wife, and their mode of life, said the Münster Anabaptists, is nowhere condemned. This was conclusive to the new lawgivers, and in July they promulgated a new marriage law permitting polygamy. The change seems to have been the cause of a storm. The smith, Heinrich Mollenheke, at the head of two hundred followers, seized the Council house and imprisoned Jan van Leiden, Knipperdolling, Rothmann, Kloprys, Slachtscaep, and Vinnen in some of the cellars. It is a singular fact that not one of the Elders appears to have been among the prisoners. However, Tilbeck, whose name comes first among the Elders, seized the gates, and marching on the insurrectionists, recovered the Council house and set the prisoners free. That the women sided with the imprisoned prophet and preachers seems evident, as they were the chief means of bringing up the artillery, a measure which decided the struggle. According to Kerssenbroick, there were several executions.

4

Hitherto the siege of Münster had been conducted by the bishop's party without much energy. But on August 24th, it was decided to summon the city to yield, and if it refused, to take it by storm. The besieged were offered their lives and an amnesty for the past. They replied that they needed no grace and would defend Münster to the last man. In truth, the

---

4. In "The Restitution" it is said, "At present, women have almost everywhere the mastery and lead men as bears are led. All the world is drowned in adultery, impurity, and whoredom. We know that the intelligent, especially the fair-minded, would not say anything to the contrary." Bouterwek, Literatur und Geschichte der Wiedertäufer, p. 30.

city was well fortified, and the Anabaptist leaders did not neglect to keep the fortifications in good repair. The ten gates were well looked after, and every precaution was taken, even the destruction of all steeples, in order to get platforms on the church towers for artillery. On the 28th, the storming commenced. The gates were bombarded for two or three days, and on the 31st, the order was given for the assault. The bishop's troops got through the outer fortifications but were met there by such a well-organized defense that they were compelled to retreat with great loss, with forty of their captains missing. Had the besieged followed up their victory, they might have taken the whole camp.

In the beginning of September, at a public assembly held in the marketplace, Dusentschur, a goldsmith from Warendorf, spoke of the danger the city was in and the necessity of electing one man to look after the common weal.

Jan van Leiden affirmed in his confession that there was no understanding between him and Dusentschur, but it is evident that he expected such a call to come to him, for he was filled with trouble lest he should desire it for his own honor and glory. He had gathered from Scripture that he was the "David" promised by the prophets. "In the last days," saith the Lord, "I will raise up my servant David"—is his summary of several passages to this effect. He besought the Lord, probably lying on the ground in the form of a cross, for that was his custom, that His Heavenly Father would speak by another prophet. Again, Dusentschur stood up and said that one among them, Jan van Leiden, should be made king. The preachers, having consulted the Scriptures, announced the proposal to the people, and as no objection was raised, the supreme authority in Münster was placed in the hands of this young Hollander. The Elders then handed over to Dusentschur the sign of their authority, the sword. The new prophet, presenting the symbol of authority to Jan, said, "Take this sword of justice, and with authority compel all people to come under your rule, and so use this sword that when Christ shall come again to judgment, you shall be able to give account to Him." Then anointing Jan, he said, "In the presence of the people of God, I call you out to be king over the new Zion."

The new monarch fell on his face to the earth and cried out, "Oh my Father, since I cannot, with my poor powers, undertake such a vast rule, since to me years and ability and experience are wanting, I betake myself to the shelter of Your grace and beseech Your help and Your powerful protection. Send to me, O Father, the same, and let Your wisdom from Your holy heaven and from the seat of Your glory come to me, that it may dwell with me and work with me, that by its aid I may know and understand what before You is acceptable and pleasing. For thus would I become worthy of this office and rule Your people with justice and equity."

The new monarchy was as much as possible modeled on that of David, of which it was conceived to be the revival. Its insignia consisted of two crowns—one imperial, the other royal— both of solid gold set with jewels. There was a golden chain, a scepter, and an orb. On the cross upon the latter were engraved the words, "Ever a King of Justice." Divara, widow of Matthysz, was raised, as another Esther, to be queen. She had a household of her own, with the rest of the royal wives dwelling with her. In Jan's own household, all the leaders had a place. Knipperdolling was next to the king, holding a sort of subordinate kingship. Tilbeck was the master of the household, and Rothmann served as the king's friend and speaker. Several counselors, a scribe, and a captain of the guard completed the ensemble. The entire character of the new institutions was at once Hebrew and histrionic, reflecting the tastes of "the Common Man" in the sixteenth century—tastes produced by living for centuries in the midst of pomps and ceremonies and by his newfound enthusiasm for the Bible.

With this great aberration came at once a spirit of servility and tyranny. But to the grave and serious men who brought about this revival of an oriental court, it no doubt appeared as the first rays of the glory about to be revealed. For the grounds of their faith, we have a precious document, of which only two copies of the original editions now exist.

"The Restitution" was composed by Rothmann, aided by Kloprys, in union with the king and the other preachers. Intended for dissemination among their sympathizers in Germany and the Netherlands, it is an official explanation of the establishment of the kingdom of David, and of the restoration of all things to their original conception as set forth in holy Scripture. Two editions were published, one in October, the other apparently in November. They were no doubt sent out by trusty colporteurs, who had to find a way through the enemy's lines.

That these were by no means complete even as late as October, 1534, is seen in the fact that all the apostles sent out from Münster in that month passed safely through them, and arrived at the towns to which they were sent.

5

"The Restitution" is treated in eighteen articles. The first speaks of the fall of all things and of their complete restoration. The history of the Kingdom of God is described as a series of falls, followed in each case by a restoration, the final fall being that of Christendom. The restoration begun by Luther has been carried forward by Melchior, Matthysz, and Jan van Leiden. Preaching in Münster was not fruitful until the people were gathered together into a holy community. Through prayer, it was seen that there was no way to such a gathering but that which Christ instituted—holy baptism. (**2** and **3**) In Münster, the old law is being restored, the Old Testament is still binding; in becoming typical it has become glorious; but it is more than type and shadow, much of it consists in promises yet unfulfilled. As God is one, holy Scripture is one, and has but one meaning, that we may know God and prove our knowledge by our works. (**4**) In Münster, the right doctrine of the coming of Christ in the flesh is being restored. The Word did not take flesh of Mary, but, according to Scripture, the Word became flesh and dwelt among us. (**5**) In Münster, the right doctrine of redemption and satisfaction, namely, that Christ died for all men, is being restored. While Papists ascribe too little to redemption, Lutherans ascribe too much. (**6**) In Münster, the right order of the doctrine of Christ is being restored: repentance, faith, baptism, following Christ in obedience, righteousness, and true holiness. (**7**) Baptism is restored in Münster. Only the discipled and believing can be truly baptized. Baptism implies, in those who submit to it, a godly resolution wholly to unite themselves to God and to yield themselves up in obedience to Him. (**8** and **9**) The true Church is being restored in Münster. Two of its necessary marks are the right knowledge of Christ in Christian faith, and the keeping alone to His words and to all that He has commanded. (**9**) Thus the true doctrine of good works necessarily flows out of the true doctrine of the Church. And it is possible to do good works because God, in giving a command, gives also the power to fulfill it. (**10**) Free will as understood at Münster is a gift of God, and men will be judged for the way they use it. (**11**) This article speaks of sin and of willful sin. In (**12**) the next, concerning the corporate communion of the saints, it is said, "From the living association of the saints, it of necessity results that we praise God with one heart and one mind, and are inclined by all sorts and every kind of service to anticipate one another's wants; therefore in Münster we have given up buying and selling, and we make no use of rent or of interest, conceiving this to be eating and drinking the sweat of the poor, that is, causing others to work that we may grow fat." (**13**) At Münster, we understand the Lord's Supper to be a memorial of Christ and a reminder that we must constantly do as He has done. Watching over one another, searching each one his own heart, we seek in true faith to show forth the Lord's death, and in true love toward one another to break bread. Then, too, we earnestly pray for sundry things, especially for our brothers and sisters who are now "parleying with the dragon." (**14, 15, 16**) At Münster, we have the right ideas on marriage, the object of which is the producing of a holy seed, who shall praise God through eternity. It is only with the rightly believing, who in heart fear God, that there can be a true marriage—those who have been baptized into Christ should renew the marriage state, that they may henceforth walk in purity. Men are more free than women in marriage and ought to have the lordship. (**17**) There is no right understanding of the Kingdom of Christ. His cross is understood, but that He shall come again, and by His servants resume His Kingdom—this men will not have. Christ will come again during the present generation. The devil has ousted Christ out of His Kingdom, and by craft become prince of this World; but it will certainly come to pass that Christ with His servants will suppress the devil and his kingdom. Then will come the day of vengeance and of comfort, when each will receive according to his desserts. Then shall there come to be one flock, one shepherd, one king, who will rule over all, and the whole creation shall be free. (**18**) In the world before and after Noah, magistrates were necessary. But this godly ordinance has become perverted and has directed and established itself against God and His Word, so that the magistracy today tracks out all that dares to boast itself Christian. Never has authority acted so unjustly and so unintelligently. No Nero, no Maximin has acted as it has done in our day; so that, in fact, this is the time of which Christ spoke when He said, "the abomination shall be in the holy place." It was, therefore, high time that such authorities should be denied, and for us at Münster, Almighty God being with us, to establish a magistracy again according to His Word. To conclude, men must now resist, for at this time Christians are permitted to draw the sword against godless authorities.

"The Restitution," though no doubt widely spread, did not produce results among the Anabaptists of the surrounding countries strong enough and general enough to overcome the severe repression almost universally put in force by the governing classes throughout the empire. It must, in fact, have increased the alarm the various rulers felt at the persistence of the Münster struggle and the sympathy shown for it by "the Common Man." Catholic and Evangelical powers alike answered the appeal of the Estates of the Lower Westphalian circles, and, sinking for a time their mutual animosity, came to the help of the bishop of Münster.

6

The new king soon experienced the uneasiness said to be the lot of one who wears a crown. His oldest and nearest friend, Knipperdolling, seems to have felt himself moved to testify against him. As far as anything can be made out of a story, evidently a gross caricature, Knipperdolling, whose prophetical character was not generally recognized, delivered a testimony against autocracy and scripturalism. If he intended more, the king's presence of mind baffled the effort. Knipperdolling was arrested and imprisoned for three days and then released.

About this time, the king held a great feast on Mount Zion, as the Dom Platz, or Cathedral Square, was now called—a feast which made such an impression on the minds of those who took part in it that the story of it has come down to us in minute detail, mixed up with what looks like legend and amplification. Jan commenced by proclaiming a general amnesty for all offences, and on the 13th of October, the whole population of Münster received an invitation to the king's supper by the sound of a trumpet. The numbers differ, but at the lowest computation, between seven and eight thousand were present. The king and queen and all the court came out of the palace in procession. The king—arrayed in a coat of silk, worked with silver thread, and a scarlet doublet, an imperial crown on his head, and wearing his chains, rings, and other insignia—was surrounded by twenty-three knights and a number of men-at-arms, clad in red and blue. The king's servants waited at the tables, where each of the guests sat in the midst of his own family. A sumptuous repast of three courses was served, after which baskets of the finest wheaten cakes were placed before the king. Jan stood up and broke the cakes, saying, "Take, eat this bread, and proclaim the Lord's death." Then the queen, a flagon of wine in her hand, rose up and said, "Take, drink this, and proclaim the Lord's death." The supper concluded, the king asked the people if they were willing to hear the Lord's will. The prophet Dusentschur then announced that twenty-seven apostles had been called to go to the four quarters of the earth to preach the doctrine of the Kingdom of Heaven as taught at Münster. Eight would go to Soest, six to Osnabrück, eight to Coesfeld, and six to Warendorf.[5] Among those deputed to Soest were Dusentschur himself and Slachtscaep, the Wassenberg preacher; among those to Osnabrück was Vinnen, another of the Wassenberg preachers, and among those to

---

5. The numbers do not agree. Kerssenbroick distinctly represents Dusentschur as saying that twenty-seven apostles were to go out of Münster, but afterwards, in detailing names and places, the number proves twenty-eight. Perhaps someone was added to the original number.

Warendorf were Kloprys and Stralen, also Münster preachers. Considering the nature of the enterprise, the act was of the same character as the sortie of Jan Matthysz, and the acceptance of such a perilous mission is a testimony to the sincerity and depth of conviction that animated the Münster Anabaptists at this time. How perilous it was we have seen: Dusentschur, Slachtscaep, Kloprys, and Stralen were executed, and in all probability, Vinnen and nearly all the others. That a solemn festival, whereat twenty-seven men, some of whom had passed many years in preaching, were called out to an apostleship of the most perilous nature, should be concluded by bloodshed is not to be credited on such testimony as that of Kerssenbroick and Ciresbeck, who both assert that the king closed the day by slaughtering an unfortunate soldier who wore the uniform of the besiegers' army. A mingling of the parables of the Great Supper and the Marriage Feast seems to have given form to the story of this memorable festival, the legend opening with going out into the streets and lanes and inviting the poor to the king's royal feast and concluding with the discovery of the man who was without the wedding garment.

Among those who went to Osnabrück was Heinrich Graess, a schoolmaster from Borcken. He fell into the hands of the bishop, and being sentenced to death, offered, in exchange for his life, to act as a spy in Münster and bring a full account of the designs of the Anabaptists, both in that city and in the rest of northwestern Germany. His offer was accepted. One morning, before the gates of the city, a man appeared in chains, asking to be let in. It was the apostle Graess, who, according to his story, had been wonderfully delivered. Neither king nor people doubted that he was a heaven-protected man, and Jan freely discussed with him all his plans. It was agreed that Graess should go to Deventer and there, on the marketplace, let "the standard fly." The king, it is said, gave him a white flag, which, when he had collected an army, he was to return flying, and the king would make a sortie to meet him. Graess left Münster but had scarcely gone beyond its horizon when he returned to his employer on January 5th, 1535. How often must the king have looked from the walls of the beleaguered city or mounted the towers and watched for the relieving armies, which he and the Münster leaders had made so many efforts to obtain. But they never came, and the nervous strain under which he and his companions had long lived was fast passing, if it had not already passed, to that point where reason is obscured like the sun on a stormy day. The defenders of Münster were clever, energetic, provident, and in all matters connected with the siege, they acted with good sense and ability. But they lived, and the king as much as anyone, in an atmosphere of dreams, visions, and revelations. They accepted optical illusions as divine signs and wonders. In this, however, they were not peculiar, for even the strongest minds of the time, such as Luther and Melancthon, did the same. One night, the king arose from his bed and ran bare-headed and bare-footed along the walls of the city, crying, "Israel, rejoice; your deliverance is at hand!"

7

Before the year 1534 closed, the inhabitants of Münster were in such dire straits that they resorted to eating their horses. In the midst of this terrible anxiety, and hearing from time to time of the failure and cruel deaths of their brothers and allies, Rothmann composed the promised work in the Restitution. If it breathes, as it certainly does, a vindictive spirit, let us remember that there are none more likely to become a prey to that spirit than the just and generous and loving, when driven mad by foul injustice and cruel wrongs. "Kill, kill, kill, kill, kill, kill" was the cry which burst from the outraged heart of King Lear, and with the Anabaptists, it was not merely a personal wrong which excited their indignation but a wrong done, as they believed, to the Divine in Man. Rothmann called his book, "A wholly consolatory witness of the Vengeance and Judgment of the Babylonian Abominations through the Community at Münster, to all true Israelites and companions of Christ scattered hither and thither." Then follows a quotation from Psalm 149:6–9. By "Babylonian," is primarily meant all that attaches itself to Rome—Rome imperial and papal—but in a more general sense, very much what John Bunyan meant by "Diabolonian." The men that sigh and cry for all the abominations done in the midst of Christendom have been awakened and prepared for this work. God has taken the weapon of destruction out of the hands of the godless; the innocent Abel shall now turn the weapon of Cain on Cain himself. "Let not your eye spare, neither have ye pity." "Babylon must receive double for all her sins."

At Münster, the Babylonian authority is overthrown, and the city consecrated; the Kingdom of God is there rising, thither should all true Israelites hasten. When the trumpet sounds, it will be too late to cross the dividing line. There were Anabaptists, and probably not a few, who doubted this spirit of vengeance and had no belief in a material and visible Kingdom of Heaven, either at Münster or elsewhere. Of such Rothmann said, "The brothers take much offence at the Münster doctrine, for as yet they know only of the suffering of Christ and are ignorant of His Kingdom and judgment. But all has its time. As the ungodly have done, so shall it be done to them again. To comprehend this, the Scripture histories must be understood. What there seems awaiting the fleshly Israel will now be gloriously accomplished. The Babylonian captivity was a type of what Christians have suffered under the abomination of the malignants. The three years and a half during which the famine prophesied by Elias lasted, multiplied by twenty make the number of the years of the captivity, after which the Temple was rebuilt; so the second captivity has continued twenty times seventy years, that is, 1,400 years, reckoning from the time the corruption of religion began to the time of the Reformation. Thus we see that the time of the restoration of the Temple is at hand. The ungodly are seized with terror, the princes and the lords will not suffer the truth, the abomination of desolation is in the holy place. Baptism, the Supper, and Marriage are desecrated. But Israel serves idols no more. As Jeremiah says, 'And their princes shall be of themselves, and their governor shall proceed from the midst of them.' Contrary to his own imaginings and to those of the whole community, God has raised up 'a scullion, the lowest servant of the servants of the Gospel,' to sit on the throne of David and to prepare by vengeance and fighting the Kingdom of the true Solomon. Who can doubt that the charge laid on this David must have its course? Therefore, are the brothers summoned to leave the city of Destruction, hazarding the loss of goods, wife, children, and life, and under the banner of God to unite at Münster in all that to which God has stirred up His Israel." Of this book, a thousand copies were printed and sent out of Münster by six colporteurs. And this closed the year 1534.

The new year opened with the publication of a new code, from which it may be inferred that the Draconian penalties enacted by the law of the Elders had been found impracticable and, except on very rare occasions, had never been enforced. Drunkenness, gambling, and lasciviousness are not to go unpunished, and for insurrection, the death penalty is still to be enforced. Otherwise, the *lex talionis* seems to find favor. Accusations not proved will render the accuser liable himself to the penalty which the accused would suffer if convicted. Anyone causing a guiltless man to be put to death will have himself to die. Several articles relating to the camp show that the discipline was strict. Relations with friendly foreigners, especially those willing to sell food, are encouraged. All interference with the will of individuals in marriage is restrained; as marriage is a free bond, and is maintained more by nature and by the bond of love than through mere words and outer ceremonies. Misrepresentations and concealments in marriage are forbidden and will be punished. No unbeliever having committed a crime shall be permitted a refuge among Christians. No Christian once fallen away can come back on repentance, except to suffer the punishment of his offense, and no brother may trade with another brother or go from one trade to another.

Jan van Leiden, it is said, now wrote a new creed, containing the Münster doctrine on marriage. He also created twelve of his followers dukes, with titles taken from the surrounding duchies and states. Policy rather than fanaticism appears to have prompted this seemingly theatrical proceeding. The king, it is said, no longer trusted the chief persons in charge of the city gates, and wanted a pretext for removing them. The people were accordingly invited to elect the dukes. According to Gresbeck, this popular election was a farce, the king, by a trick, causing his own nominees to be returned as the elected of the people. The election, following Scriptural precedent, combined an appeal to God and to the people; that is to say, the people having named their men, the decision was made by what amounted to casting lots. This method Gresbeck probably did not understand, and it appeared to him only another proof of the shameful manner in which these Dutch "sccundrels," as he called the rulers of Münster, "deluded the people."

By April, 1535, the position of the besieged had become lamentable. The women and children were crying in the streets, for they had little else to eat but grass and green vegetables.[6] The chief responsibility at this crisis, both for the defense of Münster and the maintenance of the Anabaptist cause, fell on Jan van Leiden, and it is manifestly unjust to judge a man in this position by any ordinary standard. Rightly or wrongly, a state of siege means suspension of ordinary law. And as things grew worse and worse in Münster, and as there was reason to believe there were traitors in the city, it is probable that many despotic acts, and even summary executions occurred. It is not, however, these deplorable results, but the original cause of the errors of Münster Anabaptists that it would be most profitable to discover and denounce. That cause was their reversion to the common belief of Christendom, that in the Kingdom of Heaven there were two swords—a temporal and a spiritual. After all, Jan van Leiden's use of the temporal sword was slight compared to its employment by the enemies of the Anabaptists, both before and after Münster. At this very time the besieged city was surrounded by others in which the people were kept down by flaming faggots and bloodstained scaffolds.

The treachery of Heinrich Graess had already cost Münster one of her most hopeful allies—the city of Wesel, where executions followed the traitor's revelations. And the facts related in the chapter on the Netherlands Baptists clearly show how freely the executioners were employed in the Dutch cities.

---

6. The suburbs were remarkable for the fertility of the kitchengardens, some of which were probably within the defensive outworks.

8

At the Imperial Diet of the 4th of April, held at Worms, a large sum of money was voted for the siege of Münster, and it was definitely decided that on the fall of the city the Roman Catholic Church should be restored and become again the established religion. Notwithstanding all this help, the wished-for victory might have been longer delayed, had not the author of the chief account of what happened up to this time within the city, Heinrich Gresbeck, conspired with four soldiers to steal away. Made prisoner by the besiegers, Gresbeck informed them how Münster might easily be taken through the Krenz Gate. He traced a plan of the fortifications at this part, and made a model in clay showing how the walls might be scaled without danger. At the same time another deserter, Hansen von Langenstratena traitor first to the bishop, now to the City of Münster, where he had been acting as an inspector of the fortifications—wishing to ingratiate himself with his former master, offered to place his knowledge at the disposal of the besiegers. His offer was accepted, and the bishop's war council determined to make the attempt. The city was thrown off its guard by feigned attacks, and all being ready on the night of the 24th of June, Gresbeck swam across the moat with a rope round his waist by which he drew over a wooden bridge. The scaling of the wall effected, the guards surprised, about four hundred soldiers got into the city. But in their hurry they omitted to secure their retreat, and the nearest Münster captain soon arrived and closed the gate. The besiegers now thought the attempt had failed; but meanwhile the four hundred had got as far as the Cathedral Square, but were not able to master the principal marketplace. About the middle of the night the besieged began the attack, and drove the bishop's troops back. Jan van Leiden called upon them to surrender, and for a time there was a truce. The invaders used the moment to send their standard bearer on to the ramparts to implore aid. The storming of the city now recommenced, and the bishop's soldiers not only got over the ramparts, but succeeded in passing through the Jodevelder Gate. The fight then began anew, and at last every part of the city was taken except the principal market, where the Anabaptists entrenched themselves behind wagons and made a desperate resistance. On the promise of a free escort, they at last surrendered, and the fall of Münster was complete (June 25th, 1535).

A furious massacre now commenced; no quarter was given, all were alike slaughtered, even those to whom life had just been promised. The soldiers rushed into the Council house and pitched all whom they seized out of the windows onto the spears below. The bishop's officers allowed their troops to gratify their lust for murder; and when they began to get tired of such slaughter, the execution of the prisoners began, Münster was covered with bleeding corpses, which for a long time lay unburied.

Tilbeck, taken near the Egidius Convent, was stabbed to death; Kibbenbroick was slain before his own house. What became of Rothmann no one knows. Bernard Krechting was found in the Egidius Convent; Knipperdolling was betrayed by a woman with whom he had taken refuge, near Newbridge Gate; Jan van Leiden, also betrayed, was discovered in a bastion of the Egidius Gate. These three prisoners were not, as the rest, immediately beheaded, but were reserved for a more terrible punishment. Iron collars were forged for them, and, chained to a horse soldier's saddle, they were compelled to run to Iburg. Jan van Leiden was brought before Franz of Waldeck. "Wretch," said the bishop, "thou hast thrown me and my lands into desolation." "Priest," replied the fallen king, "that is not true." After being racked, Krechting, on the 20th of January, 1536, Jan van Leiden and Knipperdolling on the 21st, they were all taken to Münster, and on the 22nd tortured to death in a manner truly diabolical. Bound to posts by iron collars, the executioners tore their flesh from their bodies with red-hot pincers, the bishop presiding over this hellish scene. The king was the first to suffer. Knipperdolling, who witnessed the horrible nature of the martyrdom, tried to kill himself by pressing his throat against his iron collar. But the torturers were determined he should not escape a single pang of the agony designed. The bodies were taken to St. Lambert's Church, where, fixed upright in iron cages, they were suspended from the tower, the cages remaining there until recent times.

Excursus on Sources

The difficulty at this point of Anabaptist history arises from the thoroughly poisoned character of the sources. Contemporary histories and documents are more or less of this character, except such of the latter as emanate from Anabaptist sources. Of contemporary writings by Anabaptists directly relating to this period, there are the works treated of by Bouterwek in his *Literatur und Geschichte der Wiedertäufer*: "*The Confession of both Sacraments*," "*The Institution*" and "*The Book of Vengeance*"; but these writings are so rare, that of the second only two of the original copies are known to exist, and of the third there is only a single transcript made in the seventeenth century. The main contemporary histories are all designedly hostile.

Three of the sources have a special character: 1. The official state statements of the examinations of the prisoners taken on the fall of the city; 2. Kerssenbroick's Geschichte der Wiedertäufer zu Münster; 3. Gresbeck's Bericht van der Wiedertaufe in Münster. The first source is similar to those upon which great part of the previous history of Anabaptism is based: confessions extracted by, or in fear of, the rack from Anabaptist prisoners. The results are partial and misleading, because the examiners had no intention to ask questions the answers to which would tell in favor of the Anabaptists; because the account of what they do say is given by those who regard them as criminal; and, lastly, because the Anabaptists, knowing that the object was to turn them into informers and betrayers of their brethren, say the very least they can.

The second source is openly partisan, the writer speaking of the party opposed to the people of Münster as 'ours.' As a Roman Catholic, and a friend of the old aristocratic-clerical party, Kerssenbroick represents in the darkest colors all that is anti-Catholic and democratic. He is for the Bishop against the City, for the Clergy against the Laity, for the Catholic Church against the Evangelicals, for the Evangelicals against the Anabaptists, for the Council against the Guilds. He hates heresy, and despises the People as the Beast with a hundred heads. To warn the authorities for all time is the express object of his book. He not infrequently suppresses the truth. These criticisms of Kerssenbroick's history are from Cornelius's "*Berichte der Augenzeugen über das Münsterische Wiedertäuferreich.*"

The third source is a writer who had more claim than Kerssenbroick to be an eyewitness, since he was in Münster during the whole period of the Anabaptist rule. Heinrich Gresbeck, joiner, landsknecht, domestic servant, went into the city because he was afraid that a little house which his mother had there might be taken from her. A Roman Catholic, without any sympathy for Anabaptist doctrine, he had himself baptized, and obtained a post of overlooker of those who did the work on the battlements. He took advantage of the trust reposed in him to drop one night over the walls, was led to the chiefs of the besieging army, who induced him to betray the city. He showed them by plans and by models in clay how to get in, and he himself prepared the way for the bishop's soldiers to enter. This is the sort of man who is our chief authority for what happened inside Münster during the siege.

Titles of Works Consulted

- Keller, L.: *Geschichte der Wiedertäufer.*

- Cornelius, C. W.: *Berichte der Augenzeugen über das Münsterische Wiedertäuferreich.*

- Kerssenbroick, H. von: *Geschichte der Wiedertäufer zu Münster.*

8

Epilogue

Though this sketch is necessarily rapid and concise, enough has been said to show the aims of early Anabaptism and its importance in European history. It was no sectarian struggle but an effort to get the reign of Justice and Truth established on earth—the true Kingdom of Heaven. Anabaptism sought the regeneration of this world, not only in one sphere but in all. The conviction that Christ, the Light of the World, was in every man, armed it with courage to attempt so great a work. The effort created a crowd of foes, powerful and remorseless.

By its fundamental doctrine predisposed to seek the unity of humanity, Anabaptism was driven by the actual state of the world into opposition to the essentially worldly—an opposition far more real and serious than that of the churches, which taught that there were two races of men: the one reprobate, the other elect. Its test, obedience to the commands of Christ, made it impossible for it to admit that those who, calling themselves Christians, yet neglected this duty, were other than rebels to the only true King. Of the men and women of goodwill who expressed their desire to obey Christ by being baptized into His death, the Anabaptists sought to form communities wherein His kingdom would be acknowledged, His laws obeyed, and a holy society formed. Those who accepted this sign of allegiance to Christ and continued to manifest their faith by obedience to His commands were, according to the Anabaptist ideal, no longer under the yoke of the world, Christ being their only Lord and Master, and none else. If they obeyed the laws of men, it was for the sake of love, and then only so far as these laws did not interfere with loyalty to Christ.

This attitude produced intense animosity in the minds of the rulers of Christendom, who saw in it a direct attack on the base of their authority. But in the degree in which the powerful persecuted the Anabaptists, the people regarded them with confidence and affection—a state of things which naturally led the powers that then were to consider Anabaptism their most dangerous foe and to resolve upon its extermination. How they accomplished their purpose has been, to some extent, related. But the persecution only served to increase the sympathy of the people with Anabaptism. Northwestern Germany and the northern Netherlands became Anabaptist in spirit. The fusion of Anabaptism and the social-democratic movement in those lands, and more or less throughout Christendom, was complete by 1535. It is difficult, if not impossible, at that time to disentangle one cause from the other. The struggle came to a head at Münster, and the World-Church triumphed.

Tragic as is the story of the Münster Kingdom, it is of enduring benefit, for it remains a beacon to warn all who believe in a Christianity that is spiritual, free, and democratic, that the world cannot be fought by the weapons of the world. And the word "weapons" is not to be confined to military arms but to be understood in a wide and general sense. The Christian churches, societies, and individuals who make the vain attempt, unless quickly arrested, as were the Münster Anabaptists, end by becoming more worldly than the world and engaging in actions that become scandals and stumbling blocks. But as simple as this lesson is, there is none more difficult to learn, and it never seemed more so than in our own strangely sophistical age.

The fall of Münster was an awful moment for Anabaptism. Having testified for their faith with a great company of martyrs, its adherents were now pilloried as criminals, for whom no torture could be too severe, no death too cruel. And the voice of Anabaptism still cries through the ages, "Is it nothing to you, all ye that pass by? Behold and see if there is any sorrow like unto my sorrow." For what can exceed the woe of those who believe themselves led by God and yet appear to fall under the power of the devil? The Anabaptists seemed to go into darkness and not into light. But it was not so. Reality—that is to say, God Himself—took the place of clouds and mists, fantasy and vision.

Anabaptism is not dead; it slumbers in the heart of the poor man and will assuredly rise again. For the voice that proclaimed liberty of conscience in Christendom, to which, therefore, we owe all that results therefrom—liberty of thought, liberty of worship, free speech, and a free press—the voice that proclaimed the common life to be of far higher importance than the individual life, the true community to be the divine unit rather than the individual, the family, or the nation—that voice cannot be hushed in any tomb or kept silent under the heavy stone of conventional religion. For that voice is not in one man only but in all. It is the eternal conscience of the universe, the light which lighteth every man, the Lamb slain from the foundation of the world. It cries for justice from all to all, for love from all to all. It knows no favorites, makes no distinctions. But all who will share the joy hidden in its sorrow must be willing to endure its conflicts and humiliations, to hang upon its cross and enter its tomb, and so to arrive at the land where justice and love reign victorious. For there is no real crown in the universe but the crown of thorns. The only head that will forever remain royal is the head of the sufferer.

For more books by Sojourner Press, visit sojournerpress.org or visit your favorite book retailer online.

***

Lewis Sperry Chafer, *The Kingdom in History and Prophecy*.

James Hall Brookes, *Till He Come*.

Peter Goeman, *The Baptism Debate: Understanding and Evaluating Reformed Infant Baptism*.

***